RIT PRESS

The Dark Night Returns: The Contemporary Resurgence of Crime Comics

RIT PRESS

The Dark Night Returns: The Contemporary Resurgence of Crime Comics

Terrence R. Wandtke

Comics Studies Monograph Series
Gary Hoppenstand, Series Editor

Narrative Structure in Comics: Making Sense of Fragments
Barbara Postema

Superheroes in Crisis: Adjusting to Social Change in the 1960s and 1970s
Jeffrey K. Johnson

The Dark Night Returns: The Contemporary Resurgence of Crime Comics
Terrence R. Wandtke

For Bella, Ripley, Griffin, and Reuben:
I hope you fight the system for all the right reasons
(as much as I hope you aren't put in jail
for all the wrong reasons).

The Dark Night Returns:
The Contemporary Resurgence of Crime Comics

RIT Press
90 Lomb Memorial Drive
Rochester, New York 14623-5604
http://ritpress.rit.edu

Book and cover design by Bruce Ian Meader
Cover image: promotional poster for *Mister X* (see p. 37)
Printed in the U.S.A.

ISBN 978-1-933360-86-7 (print)
ISBN 978-1-933360-87-4 (e-book)

Library of Congress Cataloging-in-Publication Data

Wandtke, Terrence R., author.
The Dark Night Returns:
the Contemporary Resurgence of Crime Comics/
Terrence R. Wandtke.
pages cm. – (Comics Studies Monograph Series)
Includes bibliographical references and index.
ISBN 978-1-933360-86-7 (print: alk. paper) – ISBN 978-1-933360-87-4 (e-book)
1. Comic books, strips, etc. – United States – History and criticism.
2. Crime in literature. I. Title.
PN6725.W296 2015
741.5'973 – dc23

2014035432

CONTENTS

ACKNOWLEDGMENTS

I would like to thank all those who helped with this project in large and small ways. In general, I'll state that you know who you are (thereby covering myself in case I forget any of the major players). In particular, I thank those who enabled my research, especially Randall Scott at Michigan State University and Ashley Fisher at Judson University, provided financial support, especially the Surbeck family with their research stipend, and those who gave me encouragement, especially Gary Hoppenstand and Anna Wandtke.

FOREWORD

Ink, Paper, Crime, and Punishment

As popular storytelling evolved during the nineteenth-century in the popular press, the cities in Europe and America became frequently used settings in stories featuring crime and its detection. From the earliest decades following the Industrial Revolution in the cheap story papers and penny dreadfuls of the time, lurid tales of urban criminality exerted a tremendous attraction for a working class readership for whom robbery, theft, and violence were an everyday fact of life.

With the advent of the dime novel in America and the serialized fiction periodical in England, the innovation of a new type of hero known as the amateur detective—ranging from Edgar Allan Poe's C. Auguste Dupin to Arthur Conan Doyle's Sherlock Holmes—was able to employ superior intelligence and courage to put a halt to the law-breaking shenanigans of the criminal classes. The amateur detective became an iconic protagonist in working class fiction by the end of the late-Victorian and early-Edwardian periods, attaining a similar level of influence and popularity as its rustic literary cousins, Owen Wister's fictional American cowboy and H. Rider Haggard's intrepid British adventurer, Allan Quatermain.

Following the turn of the twentieth-century and the ensuing globally catastrophic events of World War I, the popular crime narrative in America took a decidedly darker turn. The detective heroes who once employed brains over brawn now became more proficient at using their fists and guns than their cool, rational logic. Popular fiction (and other expressions of popular storytelling, such as film and story radio) is undeniably a metaphoric social mirror, sometimes distorted but nonetheless reflective of the tastes and expectations of its readership. The horrendous violence of the war and its aftermath helped to spark the creation of a new type of iconic protagonist—the hard-boiled detective. The American crime fiction pulp magazines of the 1920s began to feature a multitude of hard-boiled private investigators who were as tough and violent as the crooks they pursued, including Carroll John Daly's Race Williams and Dashiell Hammett's Continental Op.

By the time the Great Depression devastated the American economy and workforce in the 1930s, the hard-boiled gumshoe was modified into an even more violent vigilante hero who killed crooks first and asked questions later. Month after month, the fictional, apocalyptic street of New York City were overrun by pulpwood sadistic mobsters and criminal geniuses, only to be halted and destroyed by the likes of vigilante supermen such as The Shadow, Doc Savage, and The Spider, the immediate precursors of the superhero.

Thus, out of the social paranoia that framed the Great Depression, the larger-than-life superhero was born into a new mass medium: the comic book. Superman and Batman were direct (almost plagiaristic) literary descendants of Doc Savage and The Shadow. Though the economic difficulties of the 1930s were harsh on the typical working American family, they were a financial bonanza for the infant entertainment industries, including popular film, radio, television, and comics, that thrived and grew to satisfy the escapist expectations of their audiences.

Just as World War I had altered the landscape of crime fiction, World War II had a similar effect on the genre. Dark passions and illicit violence once again came to dominate in the stories of authors such as James M. Cain and Cornell Woolrich, but this time the hard-boiled P.I.'s and pulp supermen were rarely to be found. Instead, protagonists found themselves trapped by their own forbidden sexual passions, or greed, or senseless violence, or by events that simply escalated beyond their control. And thus was born noir.

Noir enjoyed a widespread following in film as well as pulp fiction. Film noir (meaning "black film," as termed by French film critics) contributed stylistic, visual techniques that supplemented and paralleled the noir tales appearing in its print counterparts, the pulp magazine and the paperback novel. Noir stories would even appear on radio and later, on television, and these cultural expressions have been discussed in depth in many excellent published studies. But, the one area of popular storytelling that seems to have been overlooked in the large body of noir studies has been the comics, the erstwhile birthplace of Superman and Batman (the latter being the seeming ideal comics noir protagonist).

The unfortunate lack of noir comics studies has, thankfully, been rectified by Terrence Wandtke in his excellent study, *The Dark Night Returns: The Contemporary Resurgence of Crime Comics*, the third volume in the Comics Monograph Series published by the RIT Press. Wandtke's book gives us a fresh and important look at the noir genre in the comics, which is a close hybrid relative of both film and pulp fiction. Wandtke skillfully demonstrates in this study that you are about to read that noir storytelling is a significant expression in one of the most vital forms of visual entertainment in our society today: the comics. He also reveals that the comics' medium is just as effective as any other entertainment form in expression the dark side of the human condition. Enjoy.

Gary Hoppenstand, Ph.D.
Series Editor

Fig. Intro.1
A noir-influenced illustration by Frank Miller, originally published by the Amateur Press Association. Untitled, APA-5, 1972.

INTRODUCTION

Crime Comics and Other Black Masks

My feeling is that the hero has now been defined by phrases like the odious one that we were all raised with—crime does not pay. Of course it pays, you schmuck.
Frank Miller [1]

The Scene of the Crime: An Overview of Crime Fiction

Case No. 1: Suspected of his partner's murder, a tough, shady, and acerbic detective begins an investigation that implicates double-dealing police as well as outlaws; he discovers only some of the answers to his questions, learns the ancient object of everyone's quest is a fake, and ultimately, turns into the police the woman he loves, more for deceiving him than for breaking the law. Case No. 2: Seduced by the wife of a client, an insurance agent stymied by the company system murders the client as part of a scheme to claim his double indemnity insurance policy; he learns that the wife meant him to take the fall for the murder, is shot by the wife as he murders her, and ultimately, confesses his crime to the insurance investigator he loves and hates in equal degrees. Case No. 3: Waking with no memory, an amnesiac with a surgically repaired and bandaged face is told by his lover that he was injured in their almost perfect scheme to kill her husband; he remembers his face is not his own (he is her husband who killed his wife's lover in the manner intended for him) and eventually kills his unfaithful wife in a jealous rage.

Taken respectively from a famous novel (*The Maltese Falcon*), film (*Double Indemnity*), and comic book ("Only Skin Deep" in *Shock SuspenStories*), these stories represent the basic elements of a genre that came to be known as crime fiction. Even though a descendent of the mystery, the crime story clearly has less to do with detection that leads to a certain solution and more to do with anxiety born of a loss of personal control.

In connection to the growth of this genre within pulp fiction and film noir, crime fiction boomed in comic books of the 1940s, seeming likely to displace the dominance of the superhero and attract older readers to the medium. However, Fredric Wertham's fear of crime comics' influence on youth led to congressional hearings, the Comics Code, and the almost complete disappearance of the genre from comic books of the 1950s, '60s, and '70s. After several fits and starts in the 1980s, crime fiction has again become a notably popular comic book genre with cultural and artistic significance, popular again at a time when comic books teeter between dubious respectability and cultural acceptance. In the midst of this recent resurgence in crime comics, the subject matter may again be crime but is distinguished by its existential preoccupations in which individual identity does not hold in a post-industrial culture. Like the crime comics of the 1940s and more obviously the 1950s, the recent boom works in concert with other media and has a significant influence on the shape of crime fiction as a whole. Flouting the freedom from Comics Code restrictions on the presentation of profanity, violence, and sex, these contemporary crime comics push the envelope further than before. In some cases, this may bring up questions about their gratuity and male-oriented sexism, but their intentional excesses may also point to a self-conscious subversion of culture. Regardless, this resurgence is reaching an increasing number of readers and, through film adaptations, viewers with crime fiction that seems notably familiar and yet strikingly different and transgressive.

Case No. 4: Seduced by a woman and her transsexual lover, a musician, on the run from the mafia, agrees to help them by stealing a pornographic film from representatives of the Catholic Church; he discovers the film features one of his new lovers (an eternally young vampire), finds himself witness to a gang rape of the transsexual lover, and ultimately, just barely escapes with his life from the explosive fire that engulfs most characters. Case No. 5: After rescuing and falling in love with a mysterious woman, a young veteran, struggling as an artist, is drugged, helpless to prevent her subsequent kidnapping. He wages a war against organized criminals to find her, uncovers a clandestine empire built on a Dr. Wertham's technology to supply genetically perfect sex slaves, and ultimately cuts a deal with those organized criminals to keep their secret in exchange for the girl and his happiness. Case No. 6: Trying to make a life as a private investigator, a former superhero, scarred by her superheroic life, is inexorably drawn into seedy cases that reveal the underbelly of the Marvel superhero universe. She is eventually forced to confront the supervillain who mentally controlled her years ago, learns from him that she may be living in a grim and gritty superhero comic book, and has to cope with an unplanned pregnancy after her one night stand with a superhero. Taken from various crime comic books (respectively, *Black Kiss*, *Sin City: Hell and Back*, and *Alias*), these stories work in ways similar to the stories of classic crime comics but clearly also contain genre-crossing, metatextual elements that revise crime fiction in significant ways.

In addition to the fact that contemporary crime comics have had a resurgence for historically complex and important reasons, these comics deserve close reading as radically subversive portraits of the American experience.

In the 1970s, Frank Miller brought a portfolio to New York City, the center of the comic book publishing universe in America. With a head filled with the crime novels of Mickey Spillane and the darkened visuals of film noir, Miller presented to publishers a portfolio filled with images depicting conventional crime stories. Every editor with whom he met instructed him to work up material with superheroes (the only material then consistently published in the comic book industry). While Miller acquiesced in this regard, he eventually became a writer as well as illustrator for the Marvel superhero comic book *Daredevil* and forcefully reintroduced a crime fiction sensibility to the comic book world. With his runs on *Daredevil* and *Batman*, superhero comic books became more grim and gritty, more noirish. And with creator-owned titles like the *Sin City* series, Miller began a revolution that resulted in comic book companies developing separate imprints for their lines of crime comics.

Although quite an important talent, Miller wasn't a genius essentially ahead of his time and shouldn't receive sole credit for the contemporary resurgence in crime comics. Nevertheless, he is one of the most prominent voices and has insisted that, despite the presence of trade collections of crime comics in Barnes and Noble, comic books still operate outside the boundaries of general respectability. This anti-institutional position certainly appeals to him and may well describe the political and aesthetic goals of recent crime comics: "I think that comics are at their best when they are provocative, and their outlaw nature is what I want to seek out in them... It's definitely been proven as an art form; I don't think we need to plead that case anymore. We don't need to keep rationalizing our existence. Now I think we're on the offensive, culturally."[2]

Due in part to the comic book's enduring dubious respectability with the general public, the crime story has found a home there once again, realizing much of the taboo-breaking potential only suggested in its early twentieth-century crime fiction origins; it seems to have subsequently achieved greater counter-cultural notoriety with narratives more fully committed to its expressions of sexuality and excessive violence. This book will explore the meaning of this notoriety and its growing appeal to creators and consumers both inside and outside the traditional mainstream comic book industry.

The Viewing of the Body: A Definition of Comic Noir

From 1946, when the term "film noir" was first put in circulation by Nino Frank, it has been considered a rather oblique term. The inexact definition of film noir may cause anxiety for some film critics, but it has long made sense to others. The films that Frank discussed were ambiguous (*The Maltese Falcon*; *Murder, My Sweet*; and *Double Indemnity*); sympathies do not fall with the detective who represents moral order but with the criminal and his or her anti-institutional attitude toward crime, and the criminal seemed to necessitate a new term. Moreover, the obliqueness of the term has allowed people to apply it to fiction, comic books, and even video games.

Now, the French word *noir* means much more than just "dark" to fans not only of American crime films in particular but also crime fiction in general. Noir often evokes a sense of crime fiction conventions ranging from the gumshoe in a trench coat to the seductress in the red dress, from the corrupt and violent authority figures to the bleak and long-shadowed urban locales. While these are merely superficial features of noir fiction, they indicate that something other than just a crime takes place in the course of contemporary crime stories. When the culture lost faith in the hopeful future of the American dream, crime fiction reflected this anxiety by moving away from "clichéd emotionalism." [3] According to Alain Silver, this "indigenous American" art form suggests not only "a dark mood in American society, but equally, almost empirically, as a black slate on which the culture could inscribe its ills and in the process produce a catharsis to help relieve them." [4]

The express concern of this book is the black slate of contemporary crime comics, a phenomenon that I'd like to call (with some precedent) *comic noir*. And as much as I'd like to celebrate the obliqueness of American crime fiction, I realize the importance of defining comic noir in order to make it a useful starting point for this study. Nevertheless, before embarking on this task, I want to clarify that my use of a term first applied to film should not imply that contemporary crime comics are derivative of the crime films of the 1940s discussed by Nino Frank. In fact, all the above-mentioned films were adapted from crime novels (and those novels probably wouldn't have been published without the popularity of mystery thrillers in pulp magazines). Trying to find a point of origin for the mystery/thriller/crime genre is difficult and nearly impossible if one tries to locate that origin in a particular medium. As will become apparent, crime fiction is the product of twentieth-century anxieties, and the twentieth century has seen endless cross-pollination between old and new media including most notably novels, comic books, and films.

The main problem with developing an easy and comprehensive definition of comic noir is the absence of crime fiction in comic books for a considerable time due to the prohibitions of the Comics Code. Although it was the genre likely to displace superheroes in comic books in the 1950s, crime comics became taboo, a part of comics history excised from the memory of the cultural mainstream. The slow (re)growth of contemporary crime comics beginning in the 1980s seems likely to again challenge the supremacy of superheroes in the American comic book marketplace. But to many contemporary fans of crime comics, the phenomenon of crime fiction has a clearer reference point in novels and film than in comic books. While this is not entirely misguided, it represents a limited knowledge of an important artistic influence on contemporary crime comic writers such as Howard Chaykin, Frank Miller, and Brian Michael Bendis. In his history of classic crime comics of the 1940s and '50s, Mike Benton initially traces crime comics back to broadsheet publications that provided details of public executions. While they combine a moral statement against crime with a love of grotesque spectacle (like the crime comics of the 1940s and '50s), the broadsheets do not wholly function as sequential narratives in traditional comics Moreover, most of what we have come to know as crime fiction grows from twentieth- and twenty-first-century ideas about individuality in relation to widespread social corruption.

Although it finds a historical precedent in the mystery genre, crime fiction is very rarely concerned with what philosopher Ernst Bloch identified as the heart of the mystery: the methodological reconstruction of a criminal event that has already occurred. Even in crime stories that involve a private investigator, knowledge of the past is only valuable insofar as it helps the overwhelmed individual deal with the pressures of the present. Crime fiction (and more particularly, crime comics) deal with criminal activity as it occurs and the ongoing pressures of a cultural system that inevitably causes crime. With a focus on post-Chandler fiction, Ronald Schwarz argues the genre presents a "vision of a society corrupted by the actions of institutions, institutions motivated by the most banal and violent of self-interests and blithely capable of crushing the purest and bravest of individuals."[5]

Critics have struggled with how to define film noir (with Mayer and McDonnell's *Encyclopedia of Film Noir*, beginning with the essay "The Problem of Film Noir"). Is film noir content, theme, or visual style? Although critics continue to argue, the simple answer that will work herein in reference to comic books is that comic noir is all three.

While comic noir always presents a story of a crime, it is ultimately the presentation of the crime in specific thematic and visual terms that distinguish it from its historical predecessor, the mystery. Again, referring to Nino Frank with the understanding that his comments on film noir apply to most American crime fiction of that era, noir is the rejection of sentimental humanism.[6]

Rather than present us with an Enlightenment Age problem/solution model, noir suggests that problems are ultimately insolvable by a system of thought made obsolete by the industrial and post-industrial ages. According to Frank, the dynamism of violence is the only thing freeing characters from the shackles of oppressive institutions that govern their lives.[7] Falling back on older orders of thought to reject the new, misogyny finds new expression even as power is more available to women, often encouraging them to co-opt the system. The loss of individuality, the bleakness of reality, and the contrast between the real and ideal is fundamentally communicated through low-key lighting, the expanse of gray, and the use of chiaroscuro contrast.

Crime (as genre) and noir (as genre) are often treated as interchangeable terms, but noir tends to have a wider application, implying a general mood and cultural critique as well. Noir is a story of a crime that explores the desperation of industrial and post-industrial life through visual design that essentializes and distorts. In an important way, classic crime comics plumb the cultural unconscious with a narrative that reveals society's delusions. In the short-lived *Johnny Dynamite*, we have a private investigator whose savage and sexual world represents the failure of the social progress toward peace and stability. In EC's notorious *Crime SuspenStories*, we have stories of spouses who hate and want to kill one another, questioning the fundamental domestic basis of both the material and idealistic American dream. Comic noir is a term that applies to many classic crime comics but more readily applies to contemporary crime comics such as those previously mentioned in this introduction: Howard Chaykin's *Black Kiss*, Frank Miller's *Sin City: Hell and Back*, and Brian Michael Bendis's *Alias*. In contemporary crime comics, we can see artists who not only dialogue more openly with noir traditions of the past but also expand the critique typically associated with noir, reworking noir with an aesthetic approach that reveals the conventions of the genre and the medium.

For instance, *Black Kiss* is a product of Chaykin's frustrations with the content limitations placed on him by his publishers, and this independently published crime/horror story is designed to contain everything prohibited by the formerly sacrosanct Comics Code.

Sin City: Hell and Back contains a drug trip experienced by the protagonist that not only doesn't end badly but also provides an improbable survey of crime comics history that clearly identifies Miller as a creator who simultaneously employs and critiques the clichés of crime fiction. *Alias* revises the hard-boiled detective as a woman who questions her life as a product of a trend in superhero/crime comics to the point that the reader also questions her salvation through violence at the end. The meaning of such self-conscious and broad-based rebellions from industry conventions are carefully explored in this book.

Typically, classic American crime fiction is marked by the inability to escape the system. Consider the story of Sam Spade's missing persons case in Dashiell Hammett's *The Maltese Falcon*. When Spade found him, the man explained that he left the life he was living because he was nearly killed by a falling beam. This near-death experience convinced him to live a life less routine, but ironically, Spade found him somewhere else living a life almost exactly the same as the life he left behind. Perhaps comic noir provides characters with an awareness of the conventions of the story in which they find themselves to accentuate the despair in one's inability to escape the system. Or perhaps comic noir provides that awareness to develop another space for the protagonist and the reader, a space that rationalizes virtue in a world that seeks to eliminate all things virtuous. As Frank Miller notes, the end of Raymond Chandler's *The Big Sleep* may be unrelentingly bleak, but Chandler also provides something else as Phillip Marlowe works to realize virtue in a world that doesn't reward virtue: "[Chandler] disguises his material. You have to read an entire Marlowe novel before you realize that Marlowe's a compulsive do-gooder. He deliberately clouds it with cynicism. Marlowe's a poet. He's a knight in dirty armor."[8]

A Criminal on the Loose: The Recent History of Crime Comics

And so, we begin with this two-part definition: noir is a story of a crime that explores the desperation of industrial and post-industrial life through visual design that essentializes and distorts. In addition, comic noir not only dialogues more openly with noir traditions of the past but also expands the critique typically associated with noir, reworking noir with an aesthetic approach that reveals the conventions of the genre and the medium. In order to survey comic noir effectively in the four chapters of this book, I have tried to balance depth and breadth. I will demonstrate that comic noir is part of a medium-crossing tradition begun in the early twentieth century, and this will form the foundation for a focus on the aesthetic approaches of six of the foremost practitioners of comic noir: Dean Motter, Howard Chaykin, Frank Miller, Brian Michael Bendis,

Brian Azzarello, and Ed Brubaker. In turn, I will determine how Motter, Chaykin, Miller, Bendis, Azzarello, and Brubaker deploy the conventions of classic crime comics in extreme and self-conscious ways to critique the history of crime fiction, the comics industry, and American culture.

Chapter One is devoted to classic crime comics of the 1940s and 1950s (and the lost years leading to the 1980s) and how the contours of classic crime comics become a springboard for the contemporary resurgence in crime comics.

Chapter Two focuses on both Dean Motter's and Howard Chaykin's work in the direct market outside the big two comic book publishers (DC and Marvel), in the 1980s, synthesizing crime fiction with genres more familiar to comic book readers, such as science fiction.

Chapter Three focuses on Frank Miller's movement from the mainstream comic book industry to independent publishing in the 1990s–from grim and gritty superhero comics to his establishment of comic noir as a genre, thereafter appealing to mainstream publishers.

Chapter Four focuses on the flourishing of comic noir as represented by creative revisions of three of the most significant contemporary crime comics writers of the 2000s, Brian Michael Bendis, Brian Azzarello, and Ed Brubaker. The order of Chapters Two, Three, and Four is not strictly chronological in that I will be discussing Frank Miller's run on *Daredevil* (1980–1982) in Chapter Three after I discuss Howard Chaykin's *American Flagg!* (1983–1988) in Chapter Two. However, it is roughly chronological, based on my claim that Miller made his great impact on comic noir with his *Sin City* work in the 1990s. Moreover, I've established useful groupings that describe the aesthetics, worldview, and impact of these various creators in these three chapters. And the conclusion will make sense of these various groups as a whole, discussing whether this "outlaw" form of comic noir can remain truly outside the law in a culture happy to embrace criminals who can make ready money with their actions.

Introduction Notes

1 Elvis Mitchell, "Frank Miller Interview on SoCal's KCRW," *Comic Book Resources*, last modified March 30, 2005, http://www.comicbookresources.com/?page=article&id=4820.

2 Charles Brownstein, *Eisner/Miller* (Milwaukie, OR: Dark Horse, 2005), 178.

3 R. Barton Palmer, *Hollywood's Dark Cinema: The American Film Noir* (New York: Twayne Publishers, 1994), 8.

4 Alain Silver and Elizabeth Ward, *Film Noir* (New York: Overlook, 1992), 1. With film noir alternately described through content, style, or mood, some critics have gone so far as to suggest that film noir is merely the product of film critics' retrospection. Although Monaco nicely summarizes this position in *John Dahl and Neo-Noir* (Paul Monaco, *John Dahl and Neo-Noir: Examining Auteurism and Genre* [Lanham, MD: Lexington, 2010], 36–37), this idea relies too much on the idea that subversion cannot come from within the system. In *Neo-Noir*, Bould, Glitre, and Tuck argue that questioning genre categories in such as way misses the point, "as if a film–or genre–exists in cultural vacuum." Mark Bould, Kathrina Glitre, and Greg Tuck, *Neo-Noir*. (London: Wallflower, 2009), 3.

5 Ronald Schwartz, *Neo-Noir: The New Film Noir Style from Psycho to Collateral* (Lanham, Maryland: The Scarecrow Press, 2005), 3.

6 Nino Frank, "A New Police Genre: The Criminal Adventure," trans. Alain Silver, *Film Noir Reader 2*, ed. Alain Silver and James Ursini (New York: Limelight Editions, 1999), 19.

7 Ibid., 18.

8 Milo George, *Frank Miller: The Interviews: 1981–2003* (Seattle: Fantagraphics, 2003), 101.

APR. No.33
CRIME DOES NOT PAY
PDC
10¢

CHAPTER 1

Classic Crime Comics and the Big Sleep

I do not believe [comic books are here to stay]...I am convinced that in some way or other the democratic process will assert itself and crime comic books will go, and with them all they stand for and all that sustains them.
Fredric Wertham[1]

How the Mystery Unfolds: A Pre-History of Classic Crime Comics

Classic crime comics of the 1940s and '50s find their most discrete point of origin in the hardboiled detective stories published in pulp fiction magazines. However, it is difficult to discuss the hardboiled detective story without mentioning its origin and, in some ways, its most obvious point of contrast: the parlor room mystery. Regularly featuring a persnickety intellectual detective who works in concert with the authorities, the parlor room mystery begins with a criminal problem and ends with the detective's parlor room solution that sets the social order aright. Regularly featuring a gun-toting private investigator in a rumpled trench coat and at odds with the authorities, the hard-boiled detective story replaces the genteel detective of the English mystery with a tough anti-hero better suited to a rough-hewn and often corrupt American context. What we see on the trajectory leading to crime comics is a systematic dismantling of an Enlightenment ideal of an orderly system that can be perfected by the incisiveness of formidable human minds; in its place is an unassailable dystopia made corrupt by various groups vying for power and propelled by largely inscrutable human desires.

This redevelopment of the mystery as the crime story took place in stages throughout the late nineteenth and early twentieth centuries within popular media such as dime novels, pulp fiction, radio shows, and film as well as comic books. Even though some of these media forms were left behind as artifacts in media history, crime comics often operated in connection with all these other media forms.
The stories portrayed in crime comics seem less devoted to the status quo of high culture and more motivated by the common anxieties of a post-World War I, post-Depression era. From Dick Tracy to Batman and on to Johnny Dynamite, the detective was less likely than ever before to decisively stem the tide of corruption in the world.

And with *The Spirit, Crime Does Not Pay*, and *Crime SuspenStories*, the psychology of criminals became more interesting and less distinguishable from the psychology of those on the "right" side of the law.

Many critics date the invention of the mystery to 1841 with Edgar Allen Poe's grisly tale of a simian murderer in "The Murders in the Rue Morgue."[2] Others will be a bit more sentimental and date it to 1887 with the advent of the classic detective Sherlock Holmes in Sir Arthur Conan Doyle's "A Study in Scarlet." (Some would also argue that we shouldn't forget the 1886 debut of the less-famous American sleuth Nick Carter in *The Old Detective's Pupil*, a clear predecessor of pulp fiction detective stories.[3]) Setting aside the debate, these potential starting points suggest the early history of the mystery is shared between the United States and the United Kingdom.

The conventions of the new and popular genre were quickly established and included the presentation of a crime whose details would be reconstructed by the detective in order to bring the criminal to justice. With order restored at the end of the story, the story works as a product of its time, embodying Enlightenment principles of progress through reason. However, the Industrial Revolution had several negative social and environmental effects that encouraged questions about the faith in reason that propelled it. Moreover, upper class intellectual biases encouraging an Enlightenment faith in progress informed the mystery only in part; from its start, the mystery also worked as an expression of more common interests with the three above-mentioned detectives debuting in new forms of popular media such as magazines and dime novels. In particular, the mystery in the United States would reach new heights of popularity with the move away from the more expensive slicks (higher-quality paper publications) to the more affordable pulps (lower quality paper publications).[4] Although terribly bland by contemporary standards, Nick Carter was a great hero of the dime novels in the 1890s, an adventurous master-of-disguise who formed a foundation for later American detectives by "being constantly waylaid, hit over the head, and otherwise thoroughly beaten up."[5] Part of this affordable fiction boom that featured heroes who lived up to popular American ideals by triumphing against impossible odds, the dime novel wouldn't last far beyond the 1910s thanks to the advent of the pulp magazine.

In the 1890s, well-educated and fairly affluent people read magazines like *Harper's* and *The Atlantic*, containing both fiction and non-fiction and printed on higher quality "slick" paper. However, technological advances enabled and economic downturns necessitated lower prices to surprising success of publishers such as Frank Munsey.

Working with the maxim that the story is more important than the paper on which it was printed, Munsey produced the all-fiction *Argosy*, filled with adventure tales and printed in cheap, rough-cut pulp stock. With a low cost and containing popular stories like those of the dime novel, pulp magazines would quickly proliferate and specialize in order to reach a wide variety of interests; titles famously included *Amazing Stories*, *Black Mask*, and *Weird Tales* among dozens of others. Famously responsive to (and therefore reflective of) public opinion, the pulps utilized a quick publication schedule and anthology format to give the public what they wanted.[6]

While it was not the only pulp devoted to mystery and crime stories (other titles among many included *Private Detective* and *Spicy Mystery*), *Black Mask* is the most often cited for several reasons. As one of the first of the pulps to be devoted solely to mystery and crime stories in 1920, *Black Mask* gathered together many authors devoted to an increasingly popular type of mystery eventually called the hard-boiled detective story. As World War I patriotism faded and unemployment grew in the early 1920s, this less optimistic and more naturalistic variation on the mystery took hold with authors such as J.S. Fletcher and Carol John Daly. With Daly's tough and sharp-tongued Race Williams, a model was established for the private investigator often seen in similar serialized mysteries for years to come. While the interiors of the magazines were printed on low-quality paper, innovations in printing allowed pulp publishers like Popular Publications to feature painted covers. These visual representations became central to the identity (and sales) of the pulps, and they are the reason why so many people had a clear image of the hard-boiled detective. When Dashiell Hammett's *The Maltese Falcon* debuted in *Black Mask* in 1929, the reader was treated to a fedora-wearing private investigator breaking the fourth wall by facing the buyer/reader and shooting through the newspaper in front of him. With *Black Mask* also featuring Raymond Chandler, the readers of the magazine became accustomed to cities built on rampant corruption (furthering the old mystery convention with a depiction of the world that made everyone as a suspect). In addition, that world was violent, and the detective was not insulated from the violence, most often investigating an on-going criminal enterprise. Negotiating his way between nefarious authorities and seductive women with hidden agendas, the private investigator found himself at odds with the law and motivated largely by self-preservation and masculine honor.[7]

With 1929 as the publication date for *The Maltese Falcon*, Dashiell Hammett (a former Pinkerton detective) was still part of the working class who felt the effects of the looming Great Depression. Working with the perception that government failed to protect common people, and only the wealthy were insulated from the economic downturn, the detective's responsibility to the law of the land became less important. Moreover, the idea of progress, so important to industrial civilization, became suspect in *The Maltese Falcon*, with the goal of the investigative quest undermined by the counterfeit falcon. And this loss of resolution can be seen even more dramatically with Raymond Chandler in the way he dealt with one big question about *The Big Sleep* from filmmaker Howard Hawks: who killed Owen Taylor (a murder victim in the novel)? Chandler said, "he hadn't the faintest idea."[8] Philosopher Ernst Bloch identifies the problem/solution model of the mystery as an outgrowth of the morality and humanism of the Enlightenment, a story with a definite ending in which all the pieces fit[9]; cultural historian Walter Ong extends this idea with his suggestion that the classic mystery is the ultimate expression of the modern literate mind, offering perfect closure. With the mystery described in these terms, the hard-boiled detective story of *Black Mask* is clearly not a classic mystery. In the essay, "The Simple Art of Murder," Chandler described his mystery story by rejecting the polite mysteries of Agatha Christie and Dorothy Sayers as exercises in puzzle-making and trickery. And he extoled the work of Hammett and identified some level of sympathy with the criminal as necessary by arguing that Hammett "gave murder back to the kind of people that commit it for reasons, not just to provide a corpse."[10] However, at times those reasons, when discovered, are far from enough to justify the crime, and the detective hero must fall back on his male sense of a fearless self to persevere.[11]

How Crime Pays: The Origin of Classic Crime Comics

In his history of *The Classic Era of American Pulp Magazines*, Peter Haining begins with the assertion that "[pulp publishers] catered to basic needs in the male psyche because their market was almost solely focused on the U.S. male."[12] While this is true in part, Erin Smith adds another layer and gives a more nuanced reading of the limited demographic data from the time in *Hard-Boiled: Working Class Readers and Pulp Magazines*. Aimed at consumers with working class incomes, the pulps developed an audience without pretensions who "find 'equipment for living'–structures, characters, scenes, and an idiom through which to make sense of their own experience."[13]

With the rise of organized crime, especially in connection with Prohibition, working class men were trying to make sense of the free hands of criminals who very effectively realized the material aspects of the American dream. And in the wake of the suffragette movement and women working during World War 1, working class men were trying to make sense of formerly stable gender roles seemingly becoming performative choices. The hard-boiled detective stories of the pulps tended to incorporate these anxieties as they provided readers with answers through "equipment for living." The hardboiled detective was not so different than the criminal but managed to maintain a certain amount of honor through amoral virtues such as quick wits and a thick hide; he contended with strong women who targeted the weakness of his sexual desire, but he compensated through violent action that established him as excessively masculine and therefore, powerful. In comics we can recognize another popular medium that begins to address these anxieties, eventually leading to Chester Gould's serial *Dick Tracy*. Newspapers were consumed by a broad swath of United States citizenry, affordable to most and (like early comic books) likely to be passed from one reader to another.[14]

The first notable success in comic strips was Richard Outcault's *Hogan's Alley*, initially running in *New York World* in 1895 and centrally concerned with the snappy comebacks of a street urchin named Mickey Dugan (otherwise known as the Yellow Kid). With social commentary that appealed to an adult readership, the Yellow Kid spawned other strips such as *Happy Hooligan* and *The Katzenjammer Kids* described by David Hajdu in *The Ten Cent Plague*: "In their earthiness, their skepticism toward authority, and delight they took in freedom,... comics offered their audience a parodic look at itself, rendered in the vernacular of caricature."[15] In the late 1920s, many of the early comic strip readers, like Chester Gould, came of age and carried on that urban tradition with serially developed stories that more directly confronted the culture and the possibilities of the medium.

Working as a cartoonist for nearly a decade, Gould debuted *Dick Tracy* in 1931 in *The Detroit Mirror*. Although there was nothing quite like it in the comic strips at that time, the popularity of pulps like *Black Mask* and novels like W.R. Burnett's *Little Caesar* undoubtedly led to the popular success of *Dick Tracy*. Following the story of a plainclothes detective, *Dick Tracy* was a new sort of mystery thriller, a police procedural, with stories that seemed to be developed in response to the news sections of the newspaper. Crime fiction authority and future writer of *Dick Tracy* Max Allan Collins writes,

"The bloody gun battles on the front page Gould transferred to his comic strip; even Tracy's 'origin' in the daily strip was boldly shocking, with Tess Trueheart's father gunned down in his delicatessen, inspiring Tracy to join the force and find his killer."[16]

Tracy was more clearly on the side of law and order than the private investigators in many *Black Mask* stories, with a loyal sweetheart named Tess Trueheart and an orphan sidekick named Junior. However, in the thirties, Tracy was tempted from the narrow path by other beautiful women, sexy and dangerous representations of the feminine as seen in the seductive Mimi (who nearly stabbed Pat Patton, a fellow police officer, to death). The strip featured graphic ends to criminals' lives ranging from machinegun fire to rabies. In contrast to later, fantastic conventions in the strip such as Tracy's wrist radio and supervillains like Flattop Jones, early enemies like Big Boy were based on Al Capone among others, seeming very real to readers in the 1930s, despite Gould's cartoonish illustrative style. In fact, certain criminals were humanized: small crimes led to larger crimes, their bosses betrayed them without a second thought, and their family lives mirrored those of "ordinary" citizens. *Dick Tracy* approximated "the public's morbid fascination with big shot gangsters" and "anticipate[d] the anticrime crusade of the early 1930s."[17] In this way, the strip approximated both the 1931 pre-code era James Cagney crime film *The Public Enemy*, about the rise of an organized criminal, and the 1935 code era James Cagney crime film *G-Men*, about the government's war on crime.[18] The conservative backlash against folk hero gangsters represented in the movement between these two Cagney films would be seen even more clearly in Dick Tracy's spy thriller imitations, *Dan Dunn* and *Secret Agent X-9* (written by Dashiell Hammett).

While the appearance of pulp magazines like *G-Men* and *The Feds* in 1936 seemed to indicate a shift in focus, their stories simply shifted focus and rearranged elements in *Black Mask* crime stories, still demonstrating a fascination with the criminal mind. While these stories may present triumphant authority figures, the authoritarian power of violence at their core developed ideas that were quite similar to those of hard-boiled detective stories; triumph and, more importantly, power resided with men who asserted themselves with guns in order to control others (not just criminals, but women, immigrants, and racial others). The rise of this type of crime story was enabled by the interplay between various media forms best seen with the famous character the Shadow debuting as a fictional radio host and then quickly adapted as a full-fledged character to pulps, novels, and comic books. When the radio narrator became a character in *The Shadow* magazine, he was portrayed by Walter Gibson as a man who fought crime though the use of fear and intimidation, utilizing disguises and maintaining a secret identity.

When *Dick Tracy* and other comic strips were successfully reprinted in book form, other comic books were developed with original material based on the anthology model of the pulps. Perhaps the most famous of these comic book anthologies would be *Detective Comics*, the title that debuted Batman, a superhero very similar to the Shadow in terms of the above stated conventions. Published by Malcolm Wheeler-Nicholson (the first person to publish a book with all original comic book content), *Detective Comics* borrowed from the pulps, specializing in adventure and hard-boiled detective stories, its most famous character before Batman being the villain Ching Lung (a stereotypical "yellow peril" character).

With his appearance in *Detective Comics* No. 27 in 1939, Bill Finger and Bob Kane's Batman would captivate readers' interest as a synthesis of the hard-boiled detective story (and other influences) with the costumed superhero story made popular in comic books with Superman in the previous year. In *Comic Book Nation*, Bradford W. Wright explains, "Finger's scripts drew heavily from lurid pulp fiction as well as Universal horror films and Warner Bros. gangster films. Kane's... heavy shadows [gave] the series a cinematic and almost expressionist look."[19] Although not initially provided with an origin, the eventually told story of Batman's youth worked as something of an antithesis of the origin of the super-powered vigilante known as Superman; in addition to his lacking superpowers, the impetus for Bruce Wayne's life as a vigilante lay not with the hope of the American dream found in Superman's country life but the failure of the American dream found in Wayne's city life. Orphaned by a mugger who shot his parents, Wayne used his considerable financial resources to build crime-fighting gadgets and hone his forensic skills. Convinced that criminals were a "superstitious and cowardly lot," Wayne donned a Bat-like costume to fight crime in his home of Gotham City. Eventually, Batman would be lightened with Wayne's ward as the young and colorful Robin, but early on, Batman stories maintained not only the detective framework but also the dark and paranoid worldview of *Black Mask* (even in Batman's more fantastic stories). In an early story entitled "Batman Versus the Vampire," which includes elements of the horror pulps such as vampires and giant bears, Batman's story is still one of the detective who unravels a crime inextricably tied to his own life in a threatening and corrupt world. After Batman apprehends Wayne's fiancée during her attempt to kill a man, Batman discovers that she was hypnotized by a crime syndicate operating outside the country. When flying to confront them, his Bat-gyro provokes horror from the general populace who view the hero's aircraft as a terrifying sign of the end times. Even though Batman would lose this edge in the World War II years (with him hocking war bonds), the crime comic would take a major step forward at that time through the more realistic crime stories in Lev Gleason's *Crime Does Not Pay*.

Crime Does Not Pay: The History of Classic Crime Comics

The 1940s were shaped by a complicated intersection of the previously mentioned post-Depression era anxieties and World War II era patriotism represented on one hand by *The Spirit* and on the other by *Captain America*. At the beginning of the 1940s, newspapers became concerned that the popularity of comic books would supplant interest in newspaper comic strips, and publisher Everett Arnold worked with Will Eisner in 1940 to create a sixteen-page supplement centrally featuring Eisner's new character, the Spirit. Although complete with a diamond mask and a back-from-the-dead origin (to capitalize on the superhero boom), the Spirit was an investigator a bit more like a gumshoe than Dick Tracy. Within the restrictions of his four-color format, Eisner created a moody crime world with long shadows and evocative cityscapes that resembled the stylized presentation of similar material in film in years to come called film noir. After his near-death at the hands of a criminal, Danny Colt set aside his previously true blue identity as a police officer to capture criminals and collect the reward money.

Along with Eisner's stylish presentation of a more morally ambiguous motivation for the lead character, *The Spirit* offered readers the dangerous woman of pulp fiction in the form of Silk Satin, P'Gell, and Sand Saref. In the story that introduces P'Gell, Eisner makes a self-conscious commentary on reader expectations for comic books by having her say, "I am P'Gell… and this is not a story for little boys!!"[20]

In addition, the Spirit often became a minor character in the strip with a story like "The Killer," a profile of a criminal caught by the Spirit (who wears a yellow Dick Tracy-like fedora); when Henry returns from the socially approved violence of World War II battlefields, he has a hard time adjusting to "ordinary" life and winds up on the wrong side of the law for shooting men who intend to harm the Spirit. Allowing the reader to literally see through Henry's eyes, this subjective perspective demonstrates the relativity in defining a person as a criminal in "modern" America, thus expanding the genre: "Eisner told human interest stories within the confines of the adventure genre… Eisner's experiments with form… resulted in an unprecedented degree of narrative density and complexity."[21]

Quite different in its orientation toward criminality (and not as complex as many other superhero comic books) was Joe Simon and Jack Kirby's *Captain America*. Borrowing from the design of the superhero the Shield, *Captain America* was a more obviously political comic book, featuring Captain America punching Adolf Hitler on the cover of its first issue (published in March 1941). Capitalizing on the growing sentiment against Hitler and eventually on American wartime patriotism, Captain America became very popular; the success of this patriotic hero encouraged changes to existing superheroes like Superman and Batman, causing them to be agents of the state more than vigilantes and robbing them of their previous relevance.

With the seeds of the eventual downturn in superhero popularity in place (seen at the end of World War II), one of the first crime comic books, *Crime Does Not Pay*, made its debut in 1942. Supposedly a realistic work that reinforces the triumph of law and order during wartime, *Crime Does Not Pay* brings back to the folk story the status of past gangsters and capitalizes on the growing popular interest in criminal psychology. Hired by Lev Gleason to revitalize two superhero titles, Charles Biro and Robert Wood instead developed the series *Crime Does Not Pay,* inspired by an MGM true crime film series of the same name. With stories of relatively graphic violence in the lives of real criminals, retailers were unsure of how to display the new comic book: with other comic books or with pulp fiction magazines.[22] Sales were initially modest but rose during postwar years: "talented artists like Dan Barry and Joe Tuska brought to the series more accomplished and illustrative styles better suited to the gritty subject matter. The postwar look and tone of *Crime Does Not Pay* clearly set it apart from superhero titles, and it avoided joining their sagging commercial fate."[23]

Identifying itself as "The First Magazine of Its Kind" and "The Magazine with the Widest Range of Appeal," *Crime Does Not Pay* was identifying itself as a new kind of comic book: reading material suitable for adults (expanding the market beyond the youth traditionally associated with comic books). Its choice of material, filled with "stories of brutality, sadism, and depravity," was justified as moral entertainment: "Since the crime stories were 'all true,' the violent lives of homicidal psychopaths could be excitingly detailed as long as they ended in punishment."[24] Typically, the covers by Biro would present crimes in progress, such as issue No. 33's on which an axe-wielding maniac prepares to kill a well-endowed woman (and the background featuring victims hung in the light of a giant moon).

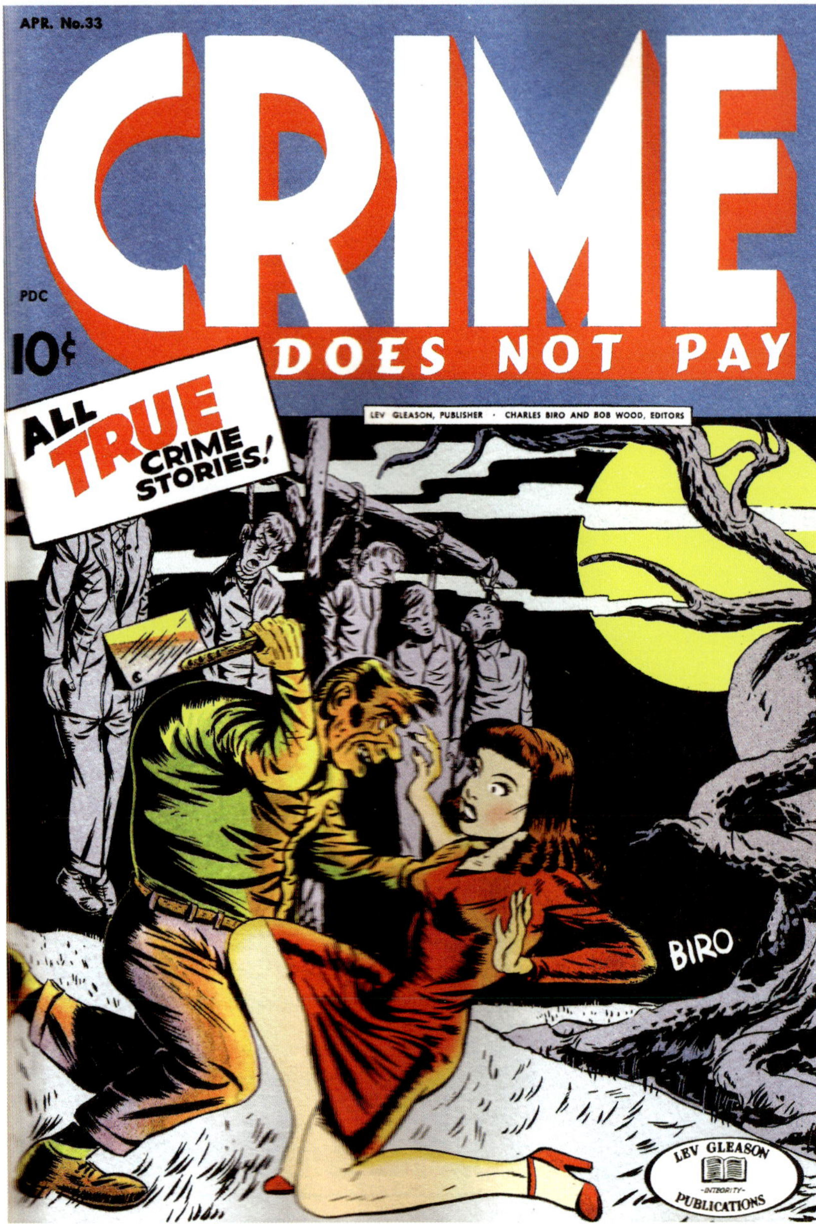

Fig. 1.1
Aberrant acts of violence were typical on the covers of *Crime Does Not Pay*
Crime Does Not Pay No. 33, Lev Gleason Publications, 1947, courtesy of Dark Horse Comics

Even more common were the covers by Biro presenting a chaotic panorama of violence created by organized criminals; for instance, issue No. 50's cover depicts a shootout between mobsters and the officers in the armored car that they encircle. One of those mobsters in the foreground is cut off in midsentence ("That's toug–") by a bullet passing through his head.

With a depiction of violence that equaled or surpassed those of the pulp covers, *Crime Does Not Pay* presented stories that generally lived up to the promise of their covers to feature "All True Crime Stories!" (a promise made in every issue). The stories portrayed criminals, usually in the big city, as they rise and fall, with the words "crime does not pay" used in the narration of the final panel. The criminals ranged from the well-to lesser-known, from John Dillinger to "Killer" Lepke, but regardless of the fame, the most frequent scene depicted in the final panel was the criminal in the electric chair. However, in the early years of the book, authorities were always late-entry characters, presented only in the stories' third act. When criminals were caught, it was rarely due to the intelligence of the law and more frequently due to the criminals' distraction by women.[25] Without exception, the criminals, their ambitious crimes, and the bizarre and self-inflicted twists of their lives dominated the book.

For instance, in issue No. 53 with "Charles Barrone, the Murderous Bully," the story begins with Carlo (Charles) as a youth, who beats up another boy over an alleyway game of craps for winning money from Carlo that Carlo stole. As he grows up, he takes what he wants through escalating violence, scarring the face of a man who looked at his girlfriend and threatening the girlfriend with the same for any misbehavior. As Carlo fails to mend his ways after several terms in prison for his excessively violent behavior as an organized criminal, his gunplay becomes more graphic and his body count includes innocent victims such as an elderly woman. Although filled with wisecracks as he shoots ("I'll give the punks something to howl about!"),[26] he demonstrates fear and weakness only when sentenced to death ("N-No! I don't want to die!").[27]As noted by Mike Benton:

> [The] stories were careful not to blame a bad childhood environment as the cause for a criminal's future actions. Kids became juvenile delinquents and then hardened criminals because of a lack of character–not opportunity... The emphasis on juvenile delinquency leading to a life of crime and punishment was part of the moral message.... On the other hand, young readers were probably secretly thrilled by stories which showed the boyhood exploits of tough gangsters.[28]

As much as Biro and Wood stacked their letters page with testimonials declaring their stories to be a moral education for young readers, it's hard to accept their story in just those terms. The oversimplified psychology of the criminal may have made criminal activity seem more aberrant but not less exciting to the creators or audience, with violence against authority figures and women depicted in startling and perhaps gratuitous detail.

Moreover, the lead story was always narrated by the not-so-realistic "Mr. Crime," a ghostly specter with a top hat, skull-topped walking cane, and imposing fangs. Invisible to the characters, he was a forerunner for the EC horror narrators such as the Crypt-Keeper who, in this case, acted as a negative guide or "evil conscience."[29] Hardly indifferent in the aforementioned "Carlo Barrone" story, Mr. Crime comments that "what especially endeared me to Carlo was the natural way he applied himself to crime."[30] At the end, after Carlo whines that he doesn't want to die, Mr. Crime's thoughts fill the last panel (featuring Carlo in the electric chair): "Well, neither did any of my pupils, Carlo! But they did–all of them! What's the difference–there will be other suckers joining my class, learning how to rob and kill!"[31] On one hand, Mr. Crime's words accentuate the inevitable, tragic end of all criminals; on the other, his gallows humor provides a distance from the tragedy, a self-conscious awareness that allows the reader to enjoy the thrill of crime and experience the existential dread of an endless parade of evildoers to come.

Although Biro and Wood may have insisted that this was far from their intention for the series, the fascination with crime and distance from its real consequences is extended with the one-page features such as the "Crime Quiz" and "This'll Kill You" (showcasing single-panel cartoons on criminal life). Regardless, sales rose quickly after the war and led to a plethora of imitations: *Justice Traps the Guilty* (by Simon and Kirby), *Crime Must Pay the Penalty* (published by Ace), and *Crime Patrol* (published by EC), among many others. On their success, Wright comments, "these crime comics… broke from the unwritten code that comic books had to offer fulfillment, affirmation, and conflict resolution… on terms established by a supposedly virtuous and progressive society… Their collective destruction of the American dream promised no easy answers."[32] Although he may overstate the case for crime comics like *Crime Does Not Pay*, this sentiment certainly paves the way for the forthcoming discussion of Bill Gaines's EC crime comics.

Fig. 1.2
Mr. Crime, the host and spirit of *Crime Does Not Pay,* uses black humor that indicts the criminal's choices but makes light of the crime
Crime Does Not Pay No. 32, Lev Gleason Publications, 1947, courtesy of Dark Horse Comics

How *SuspenStories* Pay: The Evolution of Classic Crime Comics

At roughly the same time these crime comics found their way into newspapers and comic books, writers such as Dashiell Hammett and Raymond Chandler made the transition from pulp writer to novelist. This transition garnered them more serious attention from the established literary critics of the time, and their work was more widely read. Consequently, crime novels like Dashiell Hammett's *The Maltese Falcon* (as well as James Cain's *Double Indemnity*) became source material for the Hollywood movie industry, material "demonstrating the inseparability of politics, business, and crime in the modern city."[33] Unlike the comic book industry in the 1940s, the movie industry was bound by self-imposed regulations (the motion picture production code put in place in response to several public protests in the late 1920s). As a consequence, the seminal films in the film noir tradition (such as *The Maltese Falcon*; *Murder, My Sweet*; and *Double Indemnity*) were designed to subtly subvert a system that severely limited presentations of sex and violence and demanded a respect for authority.

French critics including Nino Frank, Raymond Borde, and Etienne Chaumeton, who established and reinforced the name for this new type of crime movie, saw the films as means "to create a sense of malaise and to transmit a critique of the United States... A savage lyricism hurls us into a world of manifest decomposition, governed by dissolute living and brutality."[34] This new understanding of urban life and the city would be a supposedly unintentional part of *Crime Does Not Pay* but was an obvious part of postwar stories of *The Spirit*. However, this critique of modern city life would reach its fullest expression with Bill Gaines's reorganization of Educational Comics with titles such as *Crime SuspenStories*. Gaines inherited from his father a company better known as EC with a large debt burden and fairly unprofitable lines of Bible, science, and humor comics.[35] Turning to other genres to make the company profitable, Gaines developed several crime series in 1948 with the help of Al Feldstein: *War Against Crime* and *Crime Patrol* (formerly with the titles *International Comics* and *International Crime Patrol*).

Although these two titles can be seen as cynical attempts to capitalize on a popular trend, *War Against Crime* quickly moved beyond the narrative paradigm established by *Crime Does Not Pay*, taking advantage of the freedom then afforded to comic book storytellers. The first issue imitated several aspects of the Biro and Wood standard with "real stories from police records" that taught "how society wins its constant war on crime" with a blindfolded Justice character that served as narrator. Despite the recurring image of the electric chair again at the end of almost every leading story, mitigating circumstances were introduced to complicate the simplistic character arc of criminals in *Crime Does Not Pay*.

In *War Against Crime* No. 2, "The Crystal Ball Killer" portrays a woman who seems a typical villainess with a macabre twist as a supposed clairvoyant, "predicting" the deaths of the people she then poisons. However, her habit as a serial murderer begins at a pitiable point, with her first victim, her husband, portrayed at the beginning of the story as a man who regularly beat her. At least as significant was Feldstein's artwork, which brought to crime comics an element of depth missing in Biro's panoramas of violence.

In "The Law's Revenge" (a story narrated by the electric chair itself), Feldstein portrays the dark influence of city life on the characters; he utilizes complex perspective (looking down at figures dwarfed by an imposing city building) and lighting that creates long shadows (as the murderer tries to escape from the police into the darkness).

In addition to mirroring conventions from film noir, the series eventually includes other tales from the similarly related genre of horror with moral resolutions less clearly tied to authority figures. With horror soon to become another EC staple in the company's road to financial success, Gaines developed his *Crime SuspenStories* more clearly for adults in regard to their content and artistic merit.

Of course, hard-boiled detective fiction, regardless of artistic merit, was always written for adults in terms of content, and in 1947, Mickey Spillane produced *I, the Jury* with Mike Hammer, a character unapologetically brutal and working outside a clearly broken system. More in the crime fiction tradition of James Cain and Jim Thompson, *Crime SuspenStories* (first published in 1950) distanced itself even further from the backpedaling of *Crime Does Not Pay*, making no apologies for its portrayals of the dark side of the American dream: "EC... challenged the creative standards of the industry [and] attacked the façade of America's Cold War consensus."[36] Regularly focusing on the insatiable greed and stymied desire of its characters, *Crime SuspenStories* presented urban and suburban stories of criminal schemes gone horribly wrong, most often plotted by spouses and other ordinary people. Most important to the stories were what Bill Gaines would describe as the O. Henry twist at the end, a twist that accentuated the crime but did not always result in capture by the often ineffective and morally suspect authorities; if the criminals next door were caught, their undoing had much more to do with their own fear and paranoia.

Fig. 1.3
Shadow is used to highlight text as it represents the main characters descent into anxiety and uncertainty in "Death's Double Cross" *Crime SuspenStories* No. 1, EC, 1950

In the first issue, Al Feldstein's story "Death's Double Cross" portrays Ruth as a woman in love with Ronnie, a twin. When he initially shuns the idea of marriage, she accepts a marriage proposal from his brother, John, and begins a life of what she calls "sheer boredom."[37] When Ronnie returns from his travels, they plot John's death, with Ronnie intending to take John's place as her husband. However, after the murder is committed, Ronnie becomes John in every way, including adopting the mind-numbing routine of suburban life, making Ruth wonder if he really is Ronnie. As strange life-threatening accidents take place, she wonders whether John had learned of their plans and murdered Ronnie. In the last panel, Ruth narrates, "So you see! I think he's trying to kill me! These incidents might have been accidents… I don't know! But… what can I think? Who am I married to now?… I… don't know! Do you?"[38] Far from *Crime Does Not Pay*, which closes the story of a crime spree with the triumph of the authorities and the punishment of the criminal, this story finishes with an open ending and, regardless of your answer to her question, an intense dread of urban life.

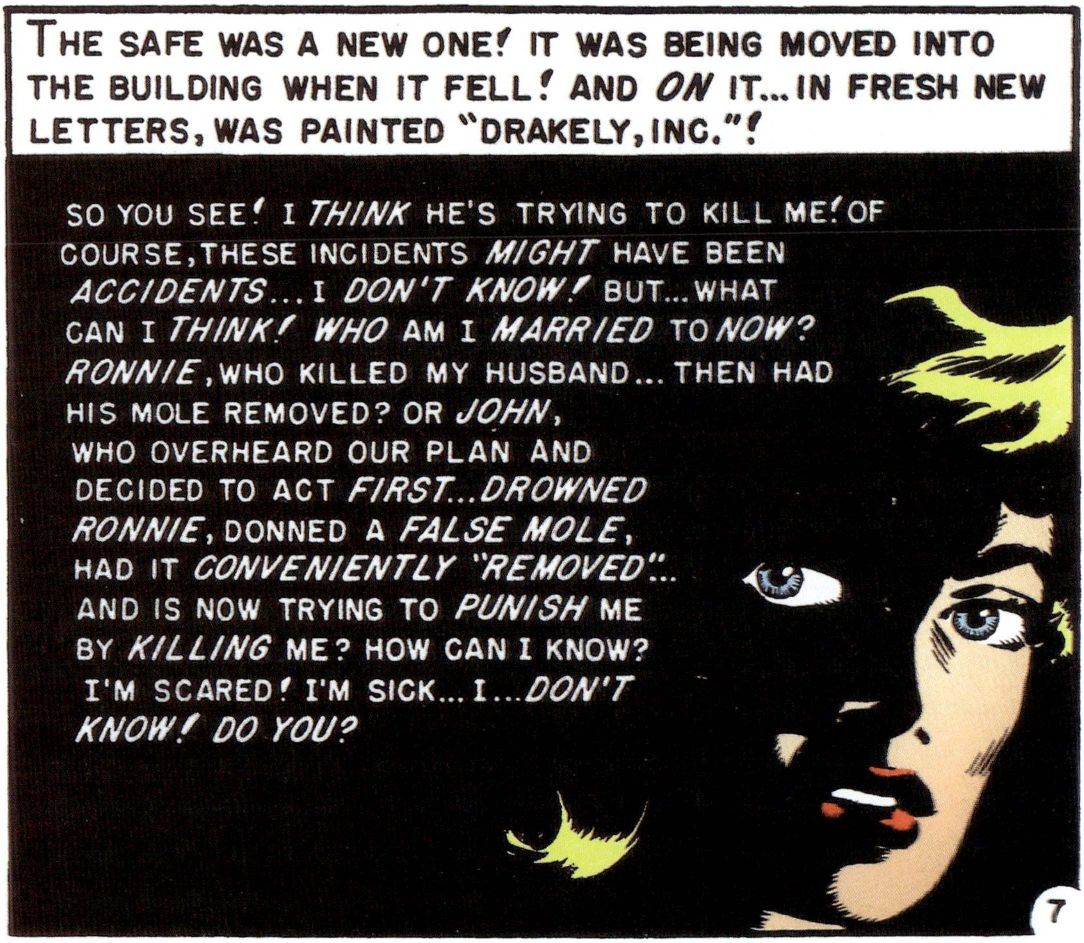

Again, these EC comics were notable for their high quality of illustration on which Gaines insisted, changing comic book publishing not only by sharing profits but also by allowing artists more time to work. The illustration in *Crime SuspenStories* contained complex line work that developed a classical sense of realism seldom seen in other comic books; perhaps more importantly, it replicated the symbolic play of light and darkness seen on the painted covers of pulps and the moving canvasses of film noir. In the last panel of "Death's Double Cross," Ruth's words are dramatically complemented by Wally Wood's clever illustration: her face, looking toward the reader but mostly obscured by the blackness that fills the entire panel. In the second issue, on the first page of "Dead Ringer," Johnny Craig portrays the oppressiveness of the protagonist's situation with a fairly unprecedented design: a man begs three others not to kill him at the bottom third of the page with the darkness of the night sky filling up all the space above and around them. He then tells his story to would-be murderers, placing the reader in a position similar to the thugs that he fears.

Fig. 1.4
A creative use of negative space to develop mood in "Dead Ringer"
Crime SuspenStories No. 2, EC, 1950–1951

Crime SuspenStories often played with perspective, giving privileged information in the politically motivated "The Execution," a story that recounts the last day of an innocent man on death row with only the reader aware that the man who throws the switch on the electric chair could exonerate him. In addition, the series played with perspective by breaking the fourth wall in "The Escaped Maniac," a story that depicts a man who picks up a hitchhiker, wrongly identifies the hitchhiker as an escaped maniac, and kills him (thus becoming a maniac who proclaims his fear of the reader as well). Perhaps most striking were the covers of *Crime SuspenStories*, eschewing the panoramic design of *Crime Does Not Pay*, focusing on a particular crime in progress, and placing the reader in the immediate space of that crime. Particularly notable was the Craig cover of No. 11, featuring the murderer carrying his new victim in the background and placing the reader behind the feet of dead bodies hanging in the cooler. Even more disturbing is No. 16 (also by Craig), which situates the reader in the defensive position of the current victim of a blade-wielding maniac.

Crime SuspenStories created a sense that the reader was not safe in the "ordinary" America of the 1950s. And as Gaines developed this series regularly engaging adult issues and artistic sensibilities, he blithely ignored the growing concerns expressed about comic books' influence on culture in general and youth culture in particular.

How *SuspenStories* Do Not Pay: The Threat to Classic Crime Comics

Cultural conservatives had been voicing concerns about comic books for many years, motivated by the shock of the new media to a system that saw comic books as a distraction from higher art. For decades, the Catholic Church had, at the diocesan level, the authority to impose bans on books that were found to be contrary to Catholic teachings. This led local churches to also make pronouncements about various forms of new media, ranging from film to comic books, that most authorities in the church did not have the expertise to evaluate. Even Bill Gaines's father, publisher of *Picture Stories from the Bible*, found himself at odds with the church in 1942 for the publication of *Sensation Comics* (featuring the scantily clad Wonder Woman).[39] Following this lead, critics became less concerned with the aesthetics of comic books (and other mass media forms) and more concerned with their perceived influence in postwar years. In *A Cycle of Outrage*, James Gilbert argues, "The dispute over mass culture in the 1950s… was shaped by the general democratization… It was a struggle in which the participants were arguing over power—over who had the right and responsibility to shape American culture. Although most participants invoked the name of all Americans, they probably thought of their fellow citizens only as passive consumers of culture, not its creators."[40]

Because superheroes defined the comic book industry for so long, initial complaints were made against Superman as a fascist role model, Wonder Woman as a feminist role model, and so on. Since women had defied stereotypes and proven capable members of the workforce during World War II, fear of the independent woman eventually became a fear of the breakdown of the traditional family and the beginning of juvenile delinquency.[41] And in an era when the Cold War resumed with added heat, prevention of juvenile delinquency had greater urgency with such action equated with the prevention of the invisible growth of Communist ideology.

Into this climate came Fredric Wertham, director of the psychiatric clinic for the New York court system, with his 1948 anti-comics article, "The Comics… Very Funny" in *The Saturday Review of Literature*. Through scant evidence that would lead to his infamous book *Seduction of the Innocent*, Wertham argued that the juvenile delinquents in his care had been shaped by the violence and sexual content of American comics, mostly crime comic books. In addition to working with an extremely limited sample and reading comic books superficially focusing on acts of violence and sex, Wertham proceeded with a simplistic cause and effect model describing the relationship between media and culture. Regardless, Wertham was not alone in his concerns (the strongest support coming from the National Education Association), and these voices mobilized the New York Legislature to enact legislation to limit comic book content.[42] After several years of study, the New York Legislature took no legal action, but concerns about comic books also received similar scrutiny in Los Angeles[43] and resulted in numerous anti-comics protests. Far from ignoring this public reaction, the Association of Comic Magazine Publishers developed a code to ban the presentation of profanity, torture, sex, and divorce as humorous, and religion and race as objects of ridicule.[44]

While most publishers broke ranks and the code never really took effect, *Crime Does Not Pay* prominently displayed this early code's seal of approval on its cover. As if sensing the impending turn of public opinion, the series thereafter presented stories that followed authority figures from the start and showed how they craftily outwitted violent (but not-too-violent) criminals. In contrast, "[n]either Gaines nor Feldstein was concerned with meeting the standards of the Association of Comic Magazine Publishers."[45]

Gaines seemed emboldened by the failure of agitators lobbying for bans in the 1950s, and he not only stayed the course but also pushed further against taboo boundaries.

In addition to *Crime SuspenStories*, EC introduced *Shock SuspenStories* in 1952, an anthology that featured a mix of crime, science fiction, and horror stories (with horror being EC's other new and popular genre in comic books). With Wertham's tendency to read for superficial content issues, he missed in EC comics what would have been most horrifying to an American public afraid of Communism: stories that humanized the criminal and criticized the system. "William Gaines and the staff at EC had both the inclination to assault the prevailing mores and conventions of mainstream America… When animated by a sense of moral outrage, EC could deliver some timely and poignant social critiques."[46] The cover of the first issue of *Shock SuspenStories* worked as a pointed contrast to the typical ending of most stories in *Crime Does Not Pay*; in the foreground, a hand is strapped to a chair and shaking from electrical current, and in the background, the witnesses look on with obvious horror at this capital punishment (with the one exception being a witness who looks on with sadistic pleasure).

Fig. 1.5
A perspective on the electric chair very different from that seen in the conventional ending of stories in *Crime Does Not Pay*
Shock SuspenStories No. 1, EC, 1952

With stories taking stands against hunting, racism, misogyny, and police brutality, *Shock SuspenStories* regularly pointed out what the EC staff considered to be institutionalized, socially acceptable evils. All of this was done within genres that EC often understood as safe vehicles for social criticism (crime, horror, and others), genres that Fredric Wertham understood as objectionable on their own terms. Undeterred by his lack of success at the state level and buoyed by the popular success of *Seduction of the Innocent*, Wertham pushed for a national hearing on comic book content. Due largely to the controversy associated with the issue and the political ambitions of Senator Estes Kefauver, the Senate Subcommittee on Juvenile Delinquency was mobilized to consider comic books and featured Wertham as its star witness.[47]

After Wertham testified, Gaines followed as the opposing star witness in defense of his work and comic books in general. In a fairly articulate opening statement, the nervous Gaines walked a line between comic books as entertainment and as art with a message and a long history, even referring to the lift of the ban on James Joyce's *Ulysses*. He extended his statement to address Wertham's critique of "The Whipping," a story of from *Shock SuspenStories* identified by Wertham as racist for using terms such as "spic" and "dirty Mexican." Establishing that it was the antagonists who used those terms in the story, he clarified that the ironic twist at the end made a clear statement against that racism.

IMPACT
AN ENTERTAINING COMIC
EC
NO.1
FEB.-MAR.
SHOCK
AUTHORIZED A. C. M. P.
CONFORMS to the COMICS CODE
10¢
SUSPENSTORIES
JOLTING TALES OF
TENSION
IN THE
EC TRADITION!
PRESS
FELDSTEIN

Despite this promising start for Gaines, it quickly became clear that the senators on the committee saw Gaines as the representation of a mass medium that would rob them of their rightful power to lead an America in crisis. Herbert Beaser focused on comic books as entertainment, and Gaines quickly backed away from his assertion that they might be regarded as art. Then, Senator Thomas Hennings asked questions about "The Orphan," another story from the same issue of *Shock SuspenStories*, in which an orphan frames her abusive foster parents for crimes and lives happily ever after. Following Wertham's line of reasoning, he suggested this meaningless entertainment was actually teaching children in similar situations to do the same (thereby, revealing the committee bias to support authority, even when abusive). Finally, Kefauver himself picked a particularly gruesome cover image from *Crime SuspenStories* No. 22 and asked Gaines whether featuring a killer holding a severed head in his hand was in good taste; Gaines asserted that it was in good taste for a horror comic book. From art to entertainment, from adult consumers to child consumers, Gaines was bullied into saying what many feared about comics. The minds of children were being polluted by the bad taste of men like Gaines who "claimed the prerogative to decide the matter on his own terms."[48]

Despite Wertham's inability to qualitatively demonstrate that crime comics or comic books in general did any harm, Gaines's testimony and the hearings overall did terrible damage to the image of the comic book industry. When the subcommittee issued their report, they were constrained by the First Amendment and placed the responsibility of policing content on the industry itself. With the negative publicity and comic book burnings accompanying these national hearings, publishers felt the need to create regulations that would strictly govern the industry and make it safe for children. Since the hearings made the medium synonymous with crime, horror, and other objectionable content that supposedly caused juvenile delinquency, the general consensus among publishers was that crime and horror comics would need to be eliminated. In *Seal of Approval*, Amy Nyberg describes this point in time: "The other publishers... were not interested in looking at what they perceived as a long-term solution. They desired more immediate action in order to stem the tide of public opinion."[49] Similar to the Hollywood production code with considerations of language use, violence, costume, sex, and depictions of religion and marriage, part A of the Comics Code made crime comics "safe" and part B made horror comics impossible.[50] Although EC continued to push boundaries and appeal to readers through 1955, sales of their crime and horror comics dropped dramatically.

In response, Gaines canceled EC's crime and horror series, in effect ending the EC line of comics (excluding *Mad* magazine) with Gaines's supposed hope of "renewed good public feelings toward comics."[51]

To clearly understand the neutering of previously adult crime narratives in comic books, the best example might be the transformation of *Johnny Dynamite*, first published by Comic Media in 1953. In comic books, Johnny Dynamite was the hardest of hard-boiled private detectives, in line with the dismal outlook and excessive violence of Mike Hammer. Most notably (evoking Hammer's ethics) in "An Eye for an Eye," Dynamite loses his eye in a shooting and when he tracks down the woman responsible, he shoots her in the belly and then in the eye as well. However, in the wake of the congressional hearings, Dynamite not only becomes honorable, respecting established laws and law enforcers; he becomes an international spy, representing the ultimate end of crime comics in the code era, replaced by the espionage thriller.

The widely accepted and enforced Comics Code made comic books safe for children and thereby conceded that the medium should be understood as a medium for children. Horror and eventually crime comic books disappeared and superhero comic books rebounded (most publishers finding the superhero story more accommodating to the changes in content mandated by the code). In the short term, this benefitted publishers such as Lev Gleason Publishers (who had already modified *Crime Does Not Pay* to fit more restrictive standards years ago) because EC was one of its primary competitors. In the long term, this benefitted publishers such as DC (named after their flagship title Detective Comics), who owned most well-known superhero properties and were well-situated to capitalize on the revival of the superhero. Regardless, the disappearance of unregulated crime comic books meant more than absence from the stands of the thrilling exploits of shady detectives, sexy women, and exciting criminals. "Reflecting a bland consensus vision of America, comic books now championed without criticism American institutions, authority figures, and middle class mores."[52] In some ways, the fearful climate of the Cold War can be blamed for the disappearance of the subversive crime story in general; *Black Mask* would cease publication in 1951, and critics would identify *Kiss Me Deadly* and *Touch of Evil* as the ultimate end and exhaustion of film noir.

However, as the pulps ceased publication, their authors and genres made their way to some respectability and paperback publication. In fact, a new generation of crime novelists such as Jim Thompson (*The Killer Inside Me*) and Patricia Highsmith (*Strangers on a Train*) continued to refine the genre in the 1950s. Film noir seemed to disappear as films made a fuller transition to color (as film noir was highly–though not entirely–reliant on its presentation in black and white). However, film noir did continue in color with crime films like *Black Widow*, *A Kiss Before Dying*, and various Alfred Hitchcock thrillers (*Rope*, *Dial M for Murder*, and *Vertigo*). In short, the willful erasure of crime comics from the developing history of comic books is exceptional, and this void has limited studies of comic books, the crime story, and U.S. culture.

The Mystery of Comic Noir: The Demise of Classic Crime Comics

Since pamphlet-style comic "books" were printed on cheap paper and considered disposable from the start, crime comic books were largely lost or destroyed in a pre-collector culture that, with the return of the superhero, forgot the popular rise of crime comics. Even though some comic book scholars may now refer to this phenomenon with interest, the crime story failed to make it into Randy Duncan and Matthew Smith's list of comic book genres in *The Power of Comics* (their textbook for comic book studies). Following the resurgence of the superhero story in the 1950s, the pulp crime and expressionist film influence on Batman was completely lost with the appearance of the campy, self-parodying Batman television series in the 1960s. And despite the supposedly establishment-challenging design of Marvel superheroes, Stan Lee borrowed from other genres like romance and science fiction and not from crime (even in the stories of less fantastic heroes like Daredevil). Crime would reappear only in fits in the subsequent decades in the taboo-breaking violence of Gil Kane's espionage comic *His Name Is… Savage* (1968), the true crime stories of Jack Kirby's prison comic *In the Days of the Mob* (1971), and the obvious allusion and content of Jim Steranko's illustrated novel *Chandler: Red Tide* (1976). For the most part, superheroes ruled and challenged the code only in very limited degrees (such as *Spider-Man* No. 96–98, ironically portraying the negative effects of drug use). As a consequence, the code was revised in 1971 to allow for such portrayals of drugs but also to allow for limited presentations of classic horror monsters such as vampires and werewolves.

DC and Marvel Comics tried to capitalize on this new freedom and created several horror-themed comic books (*I, Vampire* and *Werewolf by Night*) and also borrowed from other popular crime-related movie trends such as blaxploitation (*Luke Cage, Hero for Hire)* and kung fu films (*The Hands of Shang-Chi*). Most importantly in reference to a slight reemergence in crime comics in the 1970s was Denny O'Neil and Neal Adams's run on *Batman* in which detective work, long shadows, and lethal enemies again became important elements. However, as sharply political as O'Neil and Adams's work could be in comparison to superhero comics of the 1960s, the complex criminal stories and social critiques of a new noir aesthetic in comic books didn't fully materialize until the 1980s.

With the advent of the direct market and the industry-wide move to target adults as consumers, authors Max Allan Collins, Frank Miller, Dean Motter, Howard Chaykin, and others developed the comic noir aesthetic explored in upcoming chapters. As stated in my introduction, noir is a story of a crime that explores the desperation of industrial and post-industrial life through visual design that essentializes and distorts. Comic noir additionally not only dialogues more openly with noir traditions of the past but also expands the critique typically associated with noir, reworking noir with an aesthetic approach that reveals the conventions of the genre and the medium. With these comic noir creators, themes that first became apparent in classic crime comics form the foundation of the crime comic's resurgence of the 1980s.

First, crime comics explored moral problems through stories depicting violence with new standards of narrative and graphic realism. In worlds with potential lethal consequences for almost any action, moral problems may point to conservative solutions, but regardless of creators' intent, almost always developed a somewhat ambiguous stance toward authority and even a somewhat sympathetic attitude toward criminality. The exploration of criminal psychology and the plot twists characteristic of the genre often led to social critique and "alternative vision" for a just system in the U.S.[53]

Second, crime comics presented true stories, shaped by a particular perspective toward the truth and reality itself. The accuracy of the facts behind the "true" stories in crime comics has often been called into question, but their supposed authenticity "gave readers a vicarious thrill of horror, violence, and retribution."[54] Whether looking through the eyes of a criminal, reading narration from Mr. Crime, or understanding darkness as a thematic element, these stylized stories made their dangerous world a hyper-reality for readers.

Third, crime comics revised the optimistic view of the modern city and, like pulp fiction, replaced the optimism with a fearful worldview that saw "silent menace" everywhere.[55] Rather than providing an organized and easier life, the urban situation promised a numbing system and caused people to want to break out. Often breaking out through a sexual encounter with a seductive woman, the paranoid perspective of the male hero often was realized through his discovery of her deadly intent (thus necessitating the punishment of the nontraditional woman).

Fourth, crime comics fought a battle with social, political, and industry-based prohibitions, establishing themselves as outlaws like the criminals in crime fiction. Whether through Biro and Wood's assertion that crime comics worked for the common good or Gaines's unsuccessful testimony that crime comics should be regarded as art, these stories attempted to change industry standards. With the industry serving as a microcosm of society, crime comics initially lost in their attempt to reach a discriminating adult audience.

To different degrees (depending on the works discussed), these themes will be referenced in the analyses of three distinct phases in the development of comic noir represented in the next three chapters. Even without this resurgence of crime comics, I would characterize Fredric Wertham's bid to censor crime comics as only partly effective. Though Wertham was unhappy with Congress turning regulation of the industry back to the industry, his secondary target of superhero comics (which he also considered to be crime comics) flourished as a result of the congressional hearings. Also, due to the limitations of his focus on superficial content, Wertham missed the fact that many of the comics he read actually contained subversive messages intended to encourage readers to be agents of social change. *Seduction of the Innocent* and other works like it (such as Geoffrey Wagner's *Parade of Pleasure*)[56] are now regarded as alarmist and practically absurdist by contemporary readers. And with the resurgence of crime comics, the largely lost history of classic crime comics has again become perceived as a threat to the status quo.

In the 1980s, as neoconservatives developed a nostalgia for the simplicity of the Cold War, creators Frank Miller and Howard Chaykin used crime comics to express an urban sense of paranoia in a post-Watergate, post-Vietnam culture. Writing for an enthusiastic audience and becoming superstar comic book creators in the process, they still influence comic book creators and creators in other mediums, paving the way for crime comics to again challenge the dominance of superheroes.

Chapter 1 Notes

1 Fredric Wertham, *Seduction of the Innocent* (Laurel, New York: Main Road Books, 2004), 395.

2 In her essay "Gumshoe Gothics," Patricia Merivale traces the rudiments of both softboiled and hardboiled detective fiction back to Edgar Allen Poe's mysteries.

3 Mike Benton, *Crime Comics: The Illustrated History* (Dallas: Taylor Publishing, 1993), 97.

4 Peter Haining, *The Classic Era of American Pulp Magazines* (Chicago: Chicago Review Press, 2000), 13.

5 Tony Goodstone,
The Pulps: Fifty Years of American Pop Culture
(New York: Chelsea House, 1973), x.

6 Haining, *The Classic Era of American Pulp Magazines*, 21.

7 Ibid., 59–60.

8 Erin A. Smith,
Hard-Boiled: Working-Class Readers and Pulp Magazines
(Philadelphia: Temple University Press, 2000), 81.

9 Ernst Bloch, *The Utopian Function of Art and Literature: Selected Essays*, trans. Jack Zipes and Frank Mecklenburg (Cambridge: MIT Press, 1988), 264.

10 Raymond Chandler, *The Simple Art of Murder*
(New York: Vintage, 1988), 14

11 Smith, *Hard-Boiled*, 39.

12 Haining, *The Classic Era of American Pulp Magazines*, 9.

13 Smith, *Hard-Boiled*, 7.

14 Bradford W. Wright, *Comic Book Nation: The Transformation of Youth Culture in America*
(Baltimore: Johns Hopkins University Press, 2001), 31.

15 Ibid., 11.

16 Max Allan Collins, "*Dick Tracy* Begins,"
The Complete Chester Gould's Dick Tracy: *Dailies and Sundays 1931–1933*, by Chester Gould (San Diego: IDW, 2009), 2.

17 Benton, *Crime Comics*, 9.

18 Ibid., 12.

19 Wright, *Comic Book Nation*, 17.

20 Will Eisner, "Meet P'Gell,"
The Best of The Spirit
(New York: DC Comics, 2005), 43.

21 Randy Duncan and Matthew Smith, *The Power of Comics: History, Form, and Culture* (New York: Continuum, 2009), 15.

22 Wright, *Comic Book Nation*, 79.

23 Ibid., 79.

24 Benton, *Crime Comics*, 21.

25 Wright, *Comic Book Nation*, 84.

26 George Tuska, "Charles Barrone, the Murderous Bully," *Crime Does Not Pay* 53, Lev Gleason (July 1942), 9.

27 Ibid., 14.

28 Benton, *Crime Comics*, 25.

29 Ibid., 27.

30 Tuska, "Charles Barrone, the Murderous Bully," 2.

31 Ibid., 14.

32 Wright, *Comic Book Nation*, 84.

33 Ralph Willett, *The Naked City: Urban Crime Fiction in the USA* (Manchester: Manchester University Press, 1996), 46.

34 Raymond Borde and Etienne Chaumeton, *A Panorama of American Film Noir: 1941–1953*, trans. Paul Hammond (San Francisco: City Lights, 2002), 155.

35 David Hajdu, *The Ten Cent Plague: The Great Comic Book Scare and How It Changed America* (New York: Farrar, Straus, and Giroux, 2008), 133.

36 Wright, *Comic Book Nation*, 135.

37 Al Feldstein and Wally Wood, "Death's Double-Cross," *Crime Suspenstories* 1, EC (October–November 1950), 1.

38 Ibid., 7.

39 Hajdu, *The Ten Cent Plague*, 75.

40 James Gilbert, *A Cycle of Outrage: America's Reaction to Juvenile Delinquent in the 1950s* (New York: Oxford UP, 1986), 7.

41 Ibid., 33.

42 Amy Nyberg, *Seal of Approval: The History of the Comics Code* (Jackson: University Press of Mississippi, 1998), 37, 42.

43 Ibid., 40–41.

44 Ibid., 35.

45 Hajdu, *The Ten Cent Plague*, 142.

46 Wright, *Comic Book Nation*, 137.

47 Nyberg, *Seal of Approval*, 53.

48 Hajdu, *The Ten Cent Plague*, 272.

49 Nyberg, *Seal of Approval*, 109.

50 Ibid., 112–113.

51 Hajdu, *The Ten Cent Plague*, 288.

52 Wright, *Comic Book Nation*, 176.

53 Ibid.

54 Benton, *Crime Comics*, 49–50.

55 Willett, *The Naked City*, 6.

56 Published in 1954, Geoffrey Wagner's *Parade of Pleasure* used arguments similar to those of Fredric Wertham in his survey of film, comic books, photography, and television; in short, he found their artistic content to be sub-standard and a bad influence on youth.

. . . a point he addresses in his latest letter —
"Dear Mr. Pilgrim" — nice opening — formal — but friendly —
ust wanted to
nk you for the
d words last
y — when you
my letter and
d me, quote, a
with a mission,
te. Oh, how so
e !!!!!!" (His
asis, friends —)
"How typical of the police, to try to connect my repairs with some filthy psycho-psycho jive about some tramp."
"— and listen — repairing one of these robots — it isn't (sic) like sex —
Right! Of cour
merely a stro
fate — as luc
have it — that
EPIPHANY
— I say all —
Fix-it's "repair
— have be
performed
Devoidoid d
modeled on a
"— it's like stripping a parked car — only with legs."

CHAPTER 2

The Dark Mirror Reappears in the Future: Dean Motter and Howard Chaykin

[W]hen it comes to creating graphic amusements in the current epoch... [i]t all has to do with an honest juxtaposition of cynicism and humility.
Dean Motter

I don't believe in sweeping social change being manifested by one person, unless he has an atomic weapon.
Howard Chaykin

Dystopia in Direct Market: The Future of Comic Noir

With our initial focus on the rise of crime comics in the 1940s, it is important to not forget about the general diversity in comics before and after the 1954 Senate hearings. In addition to horror (another genre on the rise before the implementation of the Comics Code), comic book genres included teen comedy, romance, Western, jungle, war, and science fiction stories, among others. However, none captured the interest of the comic book reading public as much as the superhero comic in the 1930s and then crime stories in the 1940s. The question of how crime comics (and the comic industry) might have continued to evolve without the Comics Code is difficult to entertain due to a few other complicating factors. In the 1950s, the comic book industry would enter a recession due to the collapse of the major distributor, the American News Company. In addition, television was replete with a similar generic diversity and was "quickly dominated by large commercial interests,"[1] offering family entertainment in a more readily accessible visual media form. Regardless, with comics lines unimpeded by the limitations imposed by the Comics Code and connected to other media franchises (such as Disney cartoons and Looney Tunes), Dell Comics maintained a sizable share of the existing market for a short while.[2] But with diverse offerings that became increasingly focused on safer superhero stories, DC and Marvel maintained and increased their two large shares of the market.[3]

Despite left-leaning politics and a marketing scheme targeting an older reader, Marvel superheroes, for the most part, remained safely within Comics Code boundaries. As the popularity and cultural significance of the comic book weakened in the wake of the Comics Code, the most significant challenge to the weakening position of the medium was the comix movement of the 1960s (the underground, independently published comics that embodied the counterculture). However, the anti-institutional, boundary-pushing work of innovators like Robert Crumb had a very limited audience and therefore, a very limited effect on a medium still dominated in the U.S. by the superhero comic books of DC and Marvel.[4] The memory of other genres in comic books was largely lost as the reign of these "big two" publishers furthered the enduring association between the superhero story and the comic book. Nevertheless, distribution and technology would change in the 1980s and encourage upstart publishers to challenge the financial dominance of DC and Marvel. As stories took on more complex multi-part arcs, comic book readers skewed older, became collectors, and found a new resource in the specialty comic book stores. With better profit potential from the direct market, DC and Marvel began to focus more on these buyers and less on the old mass market venues of newsstands and drug stores. Moreover, cheaper printing technology allowed for the success of smaller publishers such as Aardvark-Vanaheim (*Cerebus*) and WaRP Graphics (*Elfquest*), who sold directly to specialty stores.[5] As these publishers' genre-bending products increased in sales, increasingly sophisticated readers took notice, which inspired other publishers. The publishers who were inspired included not only new upstarts but also the big two, creating a situation that would lead to the dramatic return of the crime comic as comic noir. While the superhero story initially continued its dominance among old and new publishers in the direct market, titles slowly began again to diversify. The crime story reappeared, but initially in indirect and variant forms through: a synthesis of the crime and science fiction story put out by new publishers in Dean Motter's *Mister X* and Howard Chaykin's *American Flagg!*; a synthesis of the crime and superhero story put out by the big two in Frank Miller's *Daredevil* and *Batman: The Dark Knight Returns*; and a female-centered hard-boiled detective story put out by a new publisher in Max Allan Collin's *Ms. Tree.*

Since the independent publishers of the 1980s didn't share the same ideological goals as the hippies of the comix generation, they didn't wholly rebel against conventional content found in comic books at the time.[6] Creators often came to new publishers still working within the conventions of the superhero story, and the publishers produced material for consumers whose tastes continued to run in line with those conventions. Superheroes and science fiction dominated the early years of the direct market along with other genres including fantasy and kung fu stories, all appealing to a predominantly male audience. Of course, many superhero stories had long been a subset of science fiction stories (dating back to Superman) but the science fiction stories that found real traction in the direct market were stories that appealed to the more sophisticated design sensibilities of more mature readers: most notably the noir science fiction of Dean Motter and Howard Chaykin. Crime stories have a long-standing relationship with science fiction, and crime and science fiction stories have long been featured side-by-side in pulp and comic anthologies.

When identifying historical precedents for what he called film noir in the seminal essay "Paint It Black: The Family Tree of Film Noir," Raymond Durgant discusses the stylistic influence of German expressionism. With long shadows and distortions of the real world representing the subjective power of the mind, German expressionist film included different genres spanning horror (*Nosferatu,* 1922), science fiction (*Metropolis,* 1927), and crime (*M*, 1931). (One of the most famous German expressionist directors, Fritz Lang, responsible for both *Metropolis* and *M*, came to the U.S. and directed well-known films noir such as *Scarlet Street* and *The Big Heat.*) Clearly working outside the utopian worldview of science fiction influenced by Enlightenment thought, *Metropolis* portrayed a future in which technology designed by a deranged genius served to exacerbate vile human impulses and dehumanize the greater part of the population. Employing typical science fiction iconography such as electrodes and bubbling beakers on their covers, the science fiction stories of pulp magazines often utilized the trope of the mad scientist driven by a power-mad, intellectual dream. As James Ursini notes in his essay "Noir Science," these images and conventions are clearly operative in the U.S.-made *Frankenstein* film with Boris Karloff. While the science fiction trend in 1950's B-movies tended to focus on cheap effects to make technology of the future, the paranoid perspective produced by "noir angst" was still part of films like *Invasion of the Body Snatchers* and television science fiction like *Twilight Zone.*[7]

The Man-Made City: Dean Motter's *Mister X*

With a futurist vision that set the standard for the subsequent, less impressive Hollywood science fiction films of the 1950s, *Metropolis* used the nightmarish template of German expressionism to render the dark underbelly of its skyscraper-filled uber-city. The technology and city design of the future did not provide citizens with a city on a hill. Instead, the imposing height of skyscrapers became the exclusive residence of the rich and powerful who callously exploit the deranged scientist at street level and the common workers below the surface. Returning to the definition established earlier, noir is a story of a crime that explores the desperation of industrial and post-industrial life through visual design that essentializes and distorts. In the early twentieth century, American hard-boiled detective fiction and film noir dealt obsessively with the psychological implications of modern civilization in the form of overgrown and dysfunctional cities. In works like Dashiell Hammett's *Red Harvest*, characters were cut free from the objectivity of an Enlightenment world and found that the supposed center of personal identity did not hold in the midst of a modern society built on lust and greed. Although setting its story in the future, *Metropolis* works in ways that represent industrial and post-industrial anxieties likewise identified in crime fiction from the 1950s. Characterizing this time in *Neon Noir*, Woody Haut states, "Noir fiction and films represent the city as a place of shadows, casual relationships and violence, where the discrepancies between the powerful and the powerless have become more obvious."[8] And looking forward to noir fiction of the 1980s, Haut identifies the way "inner cities have become virtual zones of repression."[9] In *The Naked City*, Ralph Willet references Foucault in order to describe the panoptic and paranoid sensibility of the designed city in noir;[10] moreover, the California cityspace of noir fiction intensifies this atmosphere with a highly controlled and "mediated... Disneyland lifespace."[11] Noir science fiction was material generally considered to be suitable only for pulps and B movies until the 1977 blockbuster success of *Star Wars*, George Lucas's space opera. With the way cleared for other major science fiction productions, darker visions more in line with *Metropolis* would be seen in neo-noir science fiction like Ridley Scott's *Bladerunner* in 1983.

As previously stated in reference to comix, hippy idealism in no way propelled the growth of the independent comics movement and the resurrection of crime comics. Instead, the neo-noir works of the 1980s served as an expression of a cynical culture that had internalized doubts about the authority in a post-Watergate, post-Vietnam era. Ronald Reagan's past as a Hollywood star represented to many the blatantly false hope of restoring American values because those values were never anything more than a pleasant fiction. Dean Motter's *Mister X* was part of this *Zeitgeist*, with *Metropolis* and similar futurist renderings of science fiction cities in the pulps forming the backbone of his synthesis of crime and science fiction: "I was very fixated on deco skyscraper style at the time, notably Hugh Ferris, the WPA, and Fritz Lang's *Metropolis*."[12] While the reference to Hugh Ferris (and thereby his perspective renderings of skyscrapers) is not unexpected, the mention of the Works Progress Administration is curious. A New Deal agency that employed millions of workers to carry out public works projects, the WPA represents one of the nation's largest government-based urban planning efforts. In general, urban planning as a practice in the Western world has been the product of a nineteenth-century anxiety about the unexpected disorder of industrial society, an attempt to improve cityscapes that have developed undesirable spaces like slums. Of course, the growth of the undesirable element is the fundamental nature of the city as it is understood and portrayed in classic crime fiction. Resisting the hopeful Enlightenment attitude toward the construction and management of the modern city, Motter set up his dark science fiction work to dialogue openly with noir traditions of the past. In *The Architectural Uncanny*, Anthony Vidler states, "[T]he detective novel owes its existence to… the labyrinthine spaces of the modern city… construed as the sources of modern anxiety."[13] And beginning with a single illustration of "a kind of Raymond Chandler character living in that Teutonic vision of the future," Motter thereafter drew inspiration from characters as diverse as the Spirit and Rotwang (the mad scientist in *Metropolis*). With a background as a designer, Dean Motter approached his idea like a design project and sold his idea to Vortex Comics (an innovative independent publisher) without a specific narrative in mind.

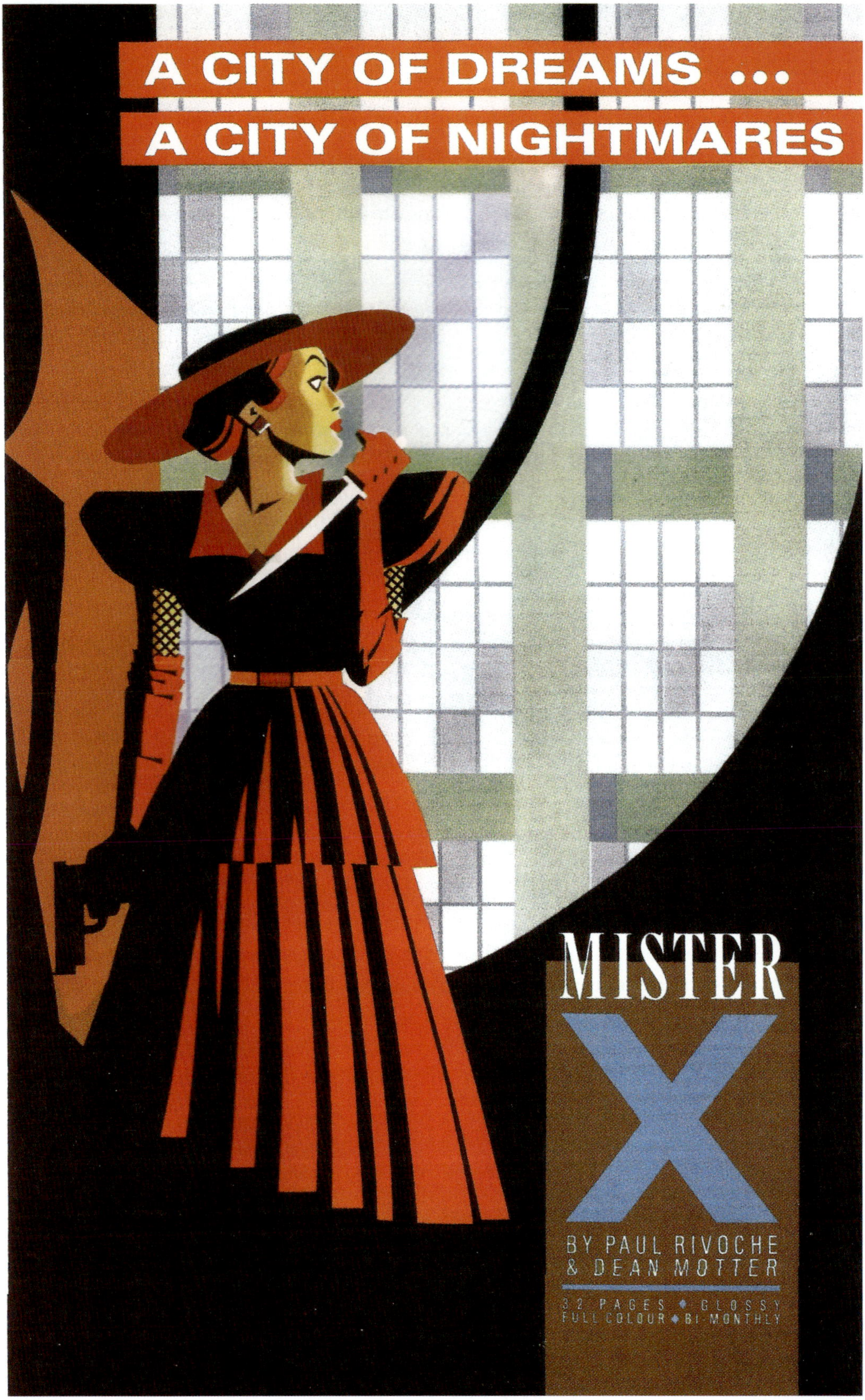
A CITY OF DREAMS ...
A CITY OF NIGHTMARES
MISTER
X
BY PAUL RIVOCHE
& DEAN MOTTER
32 PAGES ◆ GLOSSY
FULL COLOUR ◆ BI-MONTHLY

Mister X was preceded by an elaborate, year-long promotional campaign designed for the newly burgeoning direct market, making Mister X a highly recognizable character long before the first issue was plotted and sketched. Featuring a strange specter of a man with a skull-like face, the promotional posters evoked expressionism's paranoid sensibility through the distinctive noir traits such as Mister X's hard-boiled trench coat and drawn gun as well as shapely women in 1930s formalwear who casually revealed sharp knives. The same posters also evoked a strange sense of the past's vision of the future, this noir landscape filled with the skyscrapers depicted in World's Fair posters and pulp era science fiction magazines, with technology such as giant robots and brilliantly lit zeppelins made obsolete by the unfolding of time. When *Mister X* finally debuted in 1984, it clearly and self-consciously ushered in a renewed focus in comic books on city-wide corruption in a so-called civilized world, a focus often seen in the crime comics of the 1940s.

Fig. 2.1
Long shadows and the deadly woman in the red dress: conventions of noir in a promotional poster for Mister X
Mister X: The Definitive Collection, Vol. 1, Simon and Schuster, 2005 © Dean Motter

The city within the series is Radiant City, the city of the future whose landscape was portrayed in the fourteen issues of its initial run from 1984 to 1988 by Motter (as plotter and occasional writer), Jaime and Gilbert Hernandez (as writer and illustrator), and later Seth (as illustrator). Portrayed as the ultimate city planning project (designed specifically to promote benevolent city life), Radiant City has become the dramatic failure now dubbed Somnopolis. Designed by Mister X, the architecture of Radiant City, called "psychetecture," developed by Walter Eichmann and executed by Simon Myers, ironically accentuates rather than alleviates anxiety and crime as it was intended to do. Crime-ridden and filled with paranoid insomniacs who throw themselves from impossibly tall buildings, psychetecture and the great hope it represented has fallen apart. Mister X is a mysterious figure who comes into this nightmarish environment to set things right by discovering where things went wrong. Claiming to be Walter Eichmann and worried about the faulty execution of his design plans, Mister X retrieves the original design plans from mob boss Arnold Zomora and puts himself in jeopardy of the most notable criminal in Radiant City.

The City-Made Man: Dean Motter's *Mister X* Continued

The basic overview of the story seems to have a modernist sensibility à la Ayn Rand, with danger from a crime boss thrown in simply to make it more exciting. However, the mental instability of the title character makes him other than a Randian hero; injecting himself with drugs to keep awake because there is "so much to do, so little time," Mister X manifests tendencies like that of Somnopolis itself (thus casting doubt on whether Radiant City could have ever been the city he claimed or at least on whether he can fix it).

Mister X himself represents noir fears about the individual living in the midst of modern civilization. Unable to completely escape the machinations of his enemies, live without a chemical stimulant, or determine the exact details of his own life, Mister X is fundamentally estranged from his own identity. Returning from the ninth academy, an asylum/think tank, his claim to the identity of Walter Eichmann is dubious at best. He could be several other characters, and with this identity in question, he often becomes a peripheral character as people, especially the many women in his life, search for his true identity.

Even though Motter eventually saw the Hernandez brothers as having a different city sensibility than he (flatter and less futuristic),[14] their run on the series established several tropes central to the series that encapsulated Motter's futurist vision. On the first page of the first issue, Mister X ascends from the depths, essentially the position of most characters dwarfed by the oppressive verticality of Radiant City. In addition to having the city imprinted on the mirrored glasses that are the eyes of Mister X, the protagonist is regularly surrounded by the city from which he cannot be separated and through which his identity is formed.[15] The Hernandez brothers use neon outlines with art deco and modernist designs to construct a city of the future envisioned by the past; the paradox explored in the series is the inescapability of culture's firm belief in a past that never existed as the basis for its present and future sense of self.

The basic design of *Mister X*'s vision of the future is often identified as "retrofuturism" by critics and comic book creators, such as Howard Chaykin, who provides an introduction for *Mister X: Condemned*.[16] Retrofuturism describes the borrowing of imagery from classic science fiction pulps and films in order to represent an optimistic view of the future rarely seen in the dystopias of contemporary cyberpunk science fiction (for instance, William Gibson's science fiction crime novel *Neuromancer*). However, the pulps regularly added the evil genius as the human element that undermined the optimism of the future. Radiant City is anything but an easy escape into this sort of nostalgia, and Motter prefers to call his work "antique futurism,"[17] creating a greater, more obvious sense of contrast within the term. With Motter identifying the starting point for *Mister X* as "a burlesque of a gangster crime story,"[18] the series employs certain devices to make problematic the nostalgia it might evoke. The simply rendered, cartoony style of Gilbert Hernandez evokes the visual language of punch-line-driven comic strips in the 1930s, but Dick Tracy-type gangsters like Zamora are placed in a world of overt sexuality and cruelty. In one sequence, Zamora's girlfriend, Patrice, chooses a double for Mister X to play her lover as a practical joke that invites a violent reaction from the gangster's ever-present fear of her infidelity. With a triptych series of panels depicting his years as a violent thug accompanied by the text, "will the real Arnold Zamora please bear his fangs," Zamora chases and shoots at the imposter and accidentally kills one of his hired guns. The partner of the accidental victim turns his anger onto Patrice, demonstrating the deadly, labyrinthine, and indirect path of frustration so often seen in crime comics. The series often works in this way with something strangely comic (in every sense of the word)

Fig. 2.2
Although drawn in a simple style that evokes Dick Tracy, the world of *Mister X* is revealed to be far more seedy and dangerous
Mister X No. 2, Vortex, 1984 © Dean Motter

followed in short order by something both pathetic and tragic; on one page, Mister X accidentally bangs his head (with stars and a resounding "BONG"), and a friend has a mental breakdown shortly thereafter with the words, "No escape... no place to hide... We're all being murdered, you know. And this... city is the weapon. The perfect crime."[19]

Fig. 2.3
The eyes of the cityscape suggests the unavoidable surveillance of Radiant City
Mister X No. 7, Vortex, 1986 © Dean Motter

Despite the flying cars and vacuum tubes of Radiant City, Motter has a different sense of the future as "a kind of funhouse mirror of our persistent state of naïveté when it comes to technology."[20] Rather than evoking a wistfulness toward the marvel of technology, the world of *Mister X* has the feel of "broken dreams and broken promises"[21] with the "expiration date... passed for many of the technological and geopolitical advances predicted at such landmark events as the 1939 World's Fair."[22] Even though some people might regard the futurism of that event nostalgically, Motter regards it with more of a noirish cynicism, "By the time of the 1939 World's Fair, [utopianism] had been co-opted by major corporations to help sell television sets and electric dishwashers."[23] In addition to Zamora's interest in keeping Radiant City as is and Mister X's inability to separate himself from its troubles, most other commercial interests in the city are revealed as corrupt at their source. Although careful to remain within the law, Friedkin Pharmaceuticals not only develop drugs in order to capitalize on the problems of Radiant City, they also make the already drug-addicted Mister X dependent on them for a life-saving drug in order to make him part of the conspiracy to cover up their illegal activities. In this story arc, Motter suggests yet another possibility as the true identity of Mister X thanks to the investigations of Mercedes, one of many women devoted to Mister X. Already portraying Mister X as strangely ineffective and hardly masculine, the series posits something other than Zamora's tough guy as the ultimate end of the crime story of the future. This is furthered as Mercedes enters the highly exclusive Club of Sons disguised as a bearded man and looking much like Sigmund Freud. In order to entrap the Friedkin heir, she keeps the beard but opens her trench coat to reveal that she wears only lingerie. With Freud's head on a scantily clad woman's body, she highlights how the crime story's excessively constructed sexism barely keeps the unconscious and the individual's loss of control at bay, even in this antique futurist setting.

MOTTER
SETH
DIAMOND

With Seth as illustrator in this story arc, the cityscapes not only become more commercialized, like the typical city of cyberpunk, but also more symbolic. With the drug-induced fever vision of the city as a central component of the story, the city has even greater depth of field, becomes filled with eyes, and institutes the idea of reciprocal surveillance that actually makes the individual less paranoid and more vacant. This particular notion of surveillance represents a decisive loss of control in the crime fiction described by Ralph Willet in *The Naked City*: "Certain editions of this viewpoint which emphasize the dizzying, disruptive speed of urban life argue for a contemporary response which dispenses with observation and control in favor of floating through the city, numb yet euphoric."[24] The illicit pharmaceuticals of the ever-expanding Radiant City (beyond the control of its city planners) represent this attitude. Rather than a nostalgia for the modernist notion of perfect control over a city, Motter presents a neo-noir situation that makes paranoia the barely perceived norm. As the identity of the Mister X character becomes less and less certain, the series builds to a disappointing conclusion; the final issue features no direct portrayals of the character, shows only other characters in search of Mister X, and seems to end in the middle of a scene.

However, when the ibooks collected edition of the first series was published in 2005, Motter completely rewrote the final issue in an effort to explain the mysterious identity of Mister X. Even though more satisfying for fans, this version nevertheless maintained the illusory idea of identity. Setting forth the possibility that Mister X was actually L.Z. Reinhardt, a character killed in an earlier part of the series, certain facts of the series become nothing but another dream-like hallucination.[25] Making the revelation even more subversive to standard notions of identity, L.Z. Reinhardt is the *woman* who supposedly ruined Radiant City by building it with cut-rate materials. In his introduction to the second volume of the ibooks collected edition of *Mister X*, Jeffrey Morgan discusses the idea behind the term "Mister X" often used as a representation of the anonymous modern man in the 1950s: "the concept of an emblematic enigmatic outsider known only to society as Mr. X is by no means a new one."[26] Of course, this traces the source of the term to the anxieties that propelled noir fiction in that era, predicting the loss of center in individual identity for a post-industrial culture. Drawing a line from crime stories' industrial age roots to crime stories' "future," *Mister X* more fully reveals the idea of the classic crime city as seen through the self-awareness of 1980s' neo-noir science fiction.

The Hard-Boiled Patriot: Howard Chaykin's *American Flagg!*

In many ways, Howard Chaykin's *American Flagg!* is fundamentally related to *Mister X* in terms of its debut, genre-blending, and general ambition as a comic book series. First appearing in the direct market in 1983, *American Flagg!* is dystopic science fiction that elevates the medium through Chaykin's complex use of design principles; however, at its core, it is a crime story. Although not quite as concerned with city design in an explicit way, the series is set in the corrupt and commercialized Chicago of 2031, making the most of associations with the location most often featured in classic crime fiction. Chaykin's clean lines, character renderings, and art deco designs often evoke memories of early twentieth-century poster and magazine cover illustration, including recruitment posters and pin-up illustrations. However, rather than work in wholly nostalgic terms, Chaykin uses the crime story to undermine sentiment, encouraged by an upstart comic book publisher mostly separated from the Comics Code culture. Science fiction writer Michael Moorcock describes *American Flagg!* as being:

> in the tradition of the urban adventure story whose greatest exponents include Chandler, Hammer, and Phillip K. Dick. The revitalization of this form came not with the many pastiches of thirties movies and books which began to proliferate from the sixties on–a nostalgic recreation of the past that had little to do with bringing anything fresh to the genre–but with a kind of science fiction story set in the mythopoeic future as thoroughly as Chandler's stories were set in a mythopoeic Los Angles. What informed the best of these tales was what you might call a hard-nosed liberalism... an emphasis on fallible heroes and heroines.[27]

Also, in *Comics and the City,* Jorn Ahrens and Arno Meteling argue that comic books "do not only mirror different aspects of modern life, but also adopt its formal aesthetics and cultural prerequisites."[28] Perhaps more than any other aspect of the series, the innovative visual design representing the media-saturated experience of postindustrial culture is what readers were attracted to. Drawing the gaze in multiple directions with whimsy and a critical eye, Chaykin created within the reader's experience a lack of center in the all-encompassing mall-like city of the future. His innovative panel design was to become a new hallmark of comic book illustration with complex editing used to represent the post-industrial world's hostility to the individual as a linear, self-contained, and knowable construct.

At the same time, it's also worth noting some differences between *Mister X* and *American Flagg!* that inform variant ideas in the series. Located in Ontario and often associated with Dave Sim's fiercely independent Aardvark-Vanaheim, Vortex sought to elevate the comic book as art with Motter's *Mister X*, Chester Brown's *Yummy Fur*, and Ty Templeton's *Stig's Inferno*. Allowing creators to retain rights to their creations, First (the publisher of *American Flagg!*) lured some major talent from mainstream publishers; however, aside from *American Flagg!*. First produced more conventional series (including Mike Grell's spy fiction *Jon Sable* and Jim Starlin's space opera *Dreadstar*[29]). Despite some work with comic books in the 1970s, Dean Motter had been working primarily as a graphic designer when he started *Mister X* and brought to it the artistic sensibility of an outsider. After publishing in fanzines in the 1970s, Howard Chaykin worked as a creator for DC and Marvel on franchise titles as well as developing some creator-owned projects for independent publishers. Turning away from other work as a paperback cover illustrator, Chaykin came to *American Flagg!* with the intention of producing a high quality product but eschewing the high art sensibility then being developed by some publishers and creators. Happily accepting criticism from Art Spiegelman and proclaiming his love of genre fiction,[30] Chaykin positioned himself between the mainstream and the independent,[31] not necessarily keeping his inspiration at a distance. Chaykin's attitude in this regard is useful to keep in mind for this overview of *American Flagg!* Encouraged by the shift to an older comic book-reading demographic in the 1980s that enthusiastically supported the series, First allowed Chaykin, a veteran comic book creator, to gleefully explore all those things Wertham found so threatening: sex and violence, anti-heroism and government corruption, and the unorthodox visuals and panel arrangements of the medium itself. And despite Chaykin's clear critique of industrial and post-industrial culture (with an emphasis on media), he seems to often engage in loving recreations of stereotypical gender roles often portrayed in classic crime fiction and seen on covers of pulps.

American Flagg! is the story of Reuben Flagg and his crusade against the powers-that-be: governments fully integrated with multinational corporations. After "the year of the domino" (1996), in which the U.S. suffered economic failure, disease, and new economic rivals, the U.S. government relocates to Mars. With other major political powers on Mars, the U.S. government forms the Plex, a multinational corporation that runs Earth cities from Plexmalls and controls the populace with subliminal messages on television. When Flagg is replaced as an actor by a computer generated image of himself in the show *Mark Thrust, Sexus Ranger*, he joins the system in Chicago as an actual Plexus ranger. Although pleased that his image precedes him and women enthusiastically bed the man whom they see as Mark Thrust, Flagg spends his days trying to deal with widespread, systematic, and seemingly unending corruption. And while Flagg is idealistic, he is also cynical and sometimes weak; his crusade often leads him to great extremes as a sexual and violent protagonist.

Even though *American Flagg!* questions the optimistic Enlightenment view of the city much like *Mister X*, this questioning is not the main focus of the series. More important to Chaykin is the exploration of moral problems within the framework of stories depicting violence with new standards of narrative and graphic realism (ultimately leading to social critique and an "alternative vision" for a just system in the U. S.). Like Chandler, Chaykin leaned to the left in his work, but he identified a much different, much later source for his leftist politics; in the first issue of *American Flagg!*, Chaykin suggests the series was inspired by his frustration with the way the 1960s counterculture sold their beliefs in exchange for the comforts offered by corporate culture at large. Also like Chandler, Chaykin's series pushed characters and situations to extremes in ways that worked as cultural critique and sometimes even as parody of the crime story's (and its own) excessiveness.

For instance, Flagg starts his tenure as a Plex officer (a supposed extension of the established and integrated system) as someone who is shuffled aside by a computer-generated Mark Thrust (a technologically enlightened advancement of that system). In the first presentation of him as the former Mark Thrust, we see Flagg as part of a splash page, which undermines typical superheroic associations with the splash page as being a showcase of a dynamic and triumphant violent act. Instead, we see the rather ordinary and somewhat disheveled Flagg standing in front of a video presentation of a montage from *Mark Thrust, Sexus Ranger* (a fictional superhero). Flagg is surrounded by informational symbols used in the Plexmall and several text boxes that indicate time ticking until the regularly scheduled attack of an outlaw gang occurs.

GOGANG 25:40
DON'T MISS THE NEW ADVENTURES OF
MARK THRUST SEXUS RANGER
GOGANG 25:35
The provocative adventures of a fearless vice cop walking the mean streets of an unnamed, untamed and sexually transmitted-disease-riddled sector of a great urban metroplex.
starring "Reuben Flagg"
HOWARD CHAYKIN'S
AMERICAN FLAGG!
Produced entirely by Tromplography™
Brought to you each week by Consenso Research™ (you want it, you got it). A division of Am-PLEX-USA
THAT'S RIGHT, REUBEN FLAGG.
ONCE AGAIN, LIFE IMITATES ART...
...NOW CAN I GO TO BED?
GOGANG 25:28
GOGANG 25:20

With an innovative design aesthetic for the series, Chaykin reveals not only the fictions but also the consequences of an information-rich, but understanding-deprived media culture that privileges image over substance. In short order, he learns that the Plex manipulates local gangs with subliminals that cause them to attack the Plexmall, providing a justification for the Plex's consolidation of power. Moreover, the Plex's Tricentennial Recovery Committee is a cover for their plan to sell the United States to the newly emergent superpowers of the Brazilian Union of Americas and the Pan-African League. Flagg even learns that that Hilton Kreiger, the supervising officer whom he initially hates, was formerly a member of an outlaw gang who was drafted by the Plex after multiple arrests. With his new understanding of the Plex, he comes to lower his already low estimation of Krieger by seeing him as a sell-out to a corrupt (but perhaps irresistible) system.

Fig. 2.4
The initial presentation of Reuben Flagg demonstrates how his media image overshadows him and how the icons of the media world are inescapable in *American Flagg!*
American Flagg! No. 1, First, 1983

Like almost every other world in crime fiction, the people of *American Flagg!*'s Chicago find themselves becoming cogs in the system that serves only a privileged few. Much like the hard-boiled detective, Flagg finds himself in a position where he must break the law in a clandestine and sometimes violent fashion in order to genuinely serve people and see justice done.
When Krieger is murdered, Flagg's investigation reveals he was killed by John Scheiskopf (Shithead), a Plex internal affairs officer, for running a subliminal-free pirate television station. In their subsequent confrontation, Flagg lives up to a standard of crime story justice and beats Scheiskopf to near-death. Directly thereafter, with blood and vomit on his face, Flagg kisses Kreiger's daughter, Mandy, and delivers a highly idealistic speech: "The American spirit–the honest openhanded driving force of solidarity–has been castrated. Betrayed by the banks... by big business... by slimy fat cats who use patriotism like a tart uses cheap perfume... betrayed by the Plex. Someone's got to stop the decline... or try."[32] Even though idealistic, the speech still contains a hypermasculine construction of identity by referring to the castration of the American spirit and presenting a cheap tart's use of perfume as a metaphor to describe the fat cats' use of patriotism. The idealism of the speech is further mitigated by news that he left Scheiskopf in the path of one of the regular rampages of an outlaw gang (and this "vicious streak" makes him even more attractive to Mandy).

Considering the sometimes satiric tone of the series together with the sometimes excessive masculinity of Flagg, the operative question becomes how seriously to take Flagg's hard-boiled shtick. On one hand, his vicious streak undermines his idealism, but on the other, the extent of his viciousness (and its appeal to women) may also make him into an excessive noir stereotype (and thereby may undermine the viciousness itself). The possibility that not all of Flagg's characteristics may be subject to satire becomes especially important when considering his relationships with women. Throughout the series, even with his celebrity status as Mark Thrust, Flagg seems desirable to woman to an improbable degree. Regardless, in highly casual sexual relations, the looks of women in his life recall the erotic depictions of women in an era of classic crime fiction. To begin, Chaykin's illustrations of women present women in a state of undress that was often portrayed on the covers of pulp magazines; in addition, the bustier, garter belts, and stockings of the painted pin-up girls of the 1950s seem to be the undergarments of choice for all the incredibly shapely women Flagg encounters. Moreover, these women, like the noir femme fatale, often arouse Flagg's desire and weaken his resolve, representing one of the greatest of noir anxieties. Although not quite the nefarious femme fatale, Dr. Titania Weis certainly undermines the principles of Flagg as a Jewish man. As he undresses her, he is shocked to discover a swastika pendent handing from her necklace; he calls her a Nazi but she identifies a semantic change that has taken place: "Where heave you been? We're the Gotterdammercrats now… Anyway, why mix politics and sex? Besides… admit it… doesn't it give the scene… a certain edge… that turns you on… just a bit?"[33] Reuben tears the pendant from her neck and commences with their passionate encounter, thereafter calling it an act of "anger, fired by self-loathing."[34]

When reflecting on the series as a whole, Chaykin described Flagg in terms well suited to describe most protagonists in crime fiction: "He's still the basically moral guy who can be seduced by sex or power—so, he's like anybody else."[35] With temptations of sex and power as means to an end in the series, the seemingly strong women in *American Flagg!* are often treated like fetish objects whose presence merely facilitates Flagg's moral development. The letters page in *American Flagg!* featured letters from fans who addressed the potential problem within Chaykin's depiction of women in different ways. While many readers were concerned about what seemed like sexism, proponents argued the series intentionally walked a line between gratuity and cultural commentary.

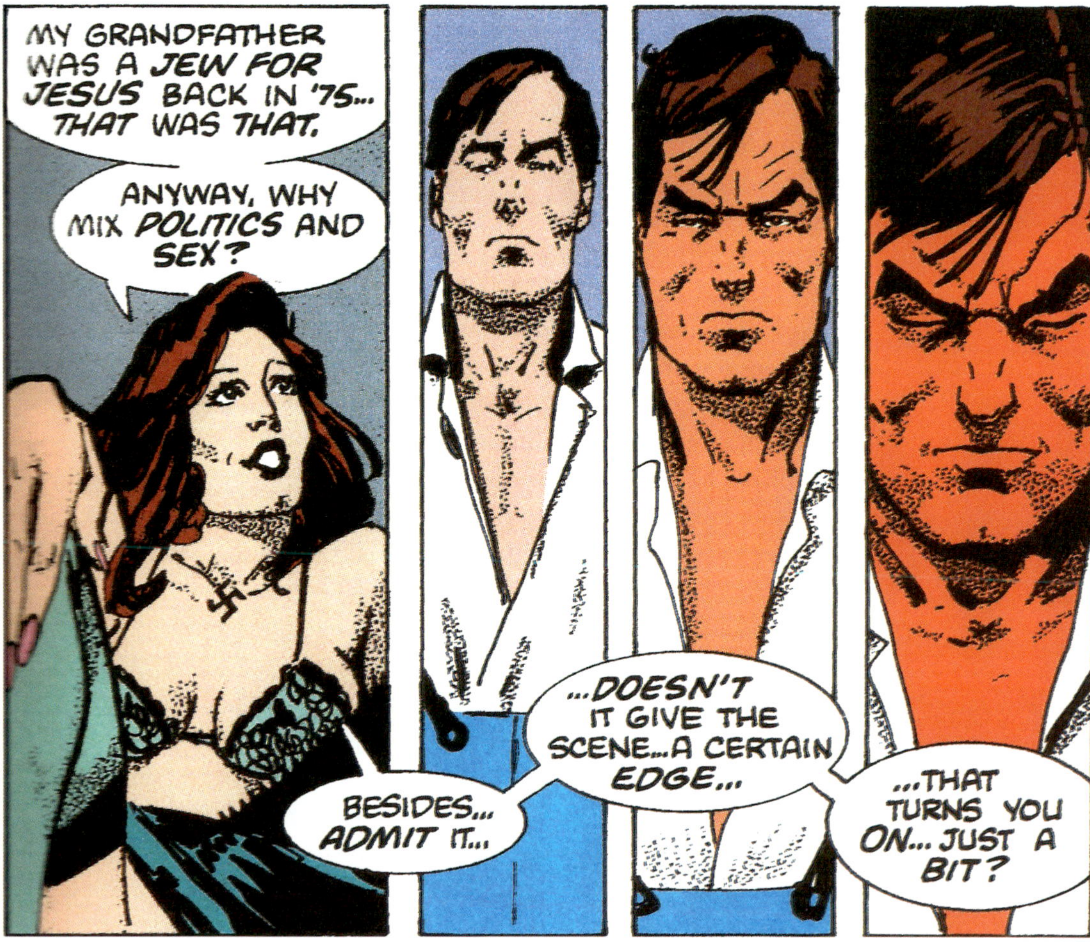

Fig. 2.5
Reuben Flagg gives into his baser desire for Titania Weis, the ultimate representation of the femme fatale for him as a Jewish character
American Flagg! No. 7, First, 1984
© Howard Chaykin.

Although Chaykin regularly stood by his series as a satire, his defense of his women in pin-up lingerie doesn't work exactly in those terms: "I don't impose my judgment on their obsessions, leave me alone with mine… [Like other popular comic books creators,] I do have an attitude of 'hey, look at those tits,' but at the same time I'm reading Simone de Beauvior, so what can I tell you? Intelligence and sex are things that have never hung together particularly well in comics and I'm trying to do my best."[36]

A New Man of Tomorrow and *Psychology Today:* Interlude

One of the most notable challenges to *American Flagg!* (and direct market comic books) would come from a 1984 *Psychology Today* article written by Professor Benjamin Demott. "Darkness in the Mall" is notably little concerned with Chaykin's comic book treatment of women, and perhaps more significant is that the article seems to miss almost all of Chaykin's biting satire. With an alarmist tone not unlike that of Fredric Wertham, Demott points out objectionable content but is really much more concerned with the supposedly pervasive "grim, self-taunting, and hopeless" attitude of direct market comic books like *American Flagg!*[37] After a profile of *American Flagg!* (with less time spent on Frank Miller's *Ronin*, Nicola Cuti's *E-Man*, and others), Demott concludes with a lament for the likely loss of American idealism, "[The] pessimism [of *American Flagg!*] remains unrelenting from start to finish... The deep, broad-based cynicism expressed and reflected in adult comics has not been a norm in this country's working class youth; its advent could have a powerful impact on politics and culture."[38] Curiously, Demott seems to have missed the widespread presence of cynicism in mainstream media in the decades following the controversy of the Watergate scandal and the Vietnam War. Likewise, he fails to recognize *American Flagg!* as part of the other popular culture trends in crime fiction, neo-noir film, and the crime science fiction blend eventually known as cyberpunk. With little popular appeal, completely unlike that of Fredric Wertham, Demott failed to excite public interest in this supposedly desperate trend that supposedly found its locus in *American Flagg!*

Despite the high profile of *Psychology Today*, his argument failed to gain traction for several likely reasons. Comic books were no longer the newest new media feared by the public at large (by then they'd been replaced by video games); comic books were no longer understood as largely read by an undiscerning youth audience; and comic books were no longer a necessary scapegoat used to expiate the enemy within our borders. Instead, the cynical comic noir aesthetic of *American Flagg!* approximated a much more widespread cultural attitude held among adults who no longer made the sharp distinction between high and low culture and no longer agreed with Demott that comic books were "proof of the onset of mass adult illiteracy."[39]

In fact, two years later, the *Atlantic Monthly* published "Comic Books for Grown-Ups," by Lloyd Rose in which *American Flagg!* was regarded in much more laudatory terms alongside Frank Miller's *The Dark Knight Returns* and Dave Sim's *Cerebus*. With much more attention paid to its satire, Rose describes the critique employed in *American Flagg!* (very similar to the standard critique employed in the crime story): "This is a shallow parody of America, exactly what people mean when they use comic book as a disparaging adjective... The shallowness is part of the point. It plays to our worst fears about our plastic, violent culture, with its philistine tastes and hunger for novelty."[40] Rose interestingly ties the pointed critique of America to the medium of the comic book itself and may suggest that Chaykin's comic book design innovations are born from the medium's enduring outsider status. With this in mind, Rose ends his article with a description of comic books that undermines them as art but sets them up as great outlaws:

With *American Flagg!* and other adult comics of the period, "[w]e're in a subaesthetic area, with no redeeming intellectual or social qualities, only instinct and rude energy."[41] Working with the same idea but in a way much more sympathetic to comic books as a medium, Bradford Wright described *American Flagg!* in this way: "Littered throughout the series were references to American junk culture: shopping malls, porn films, 'B' movies, and, naturally, comic books. With his own affection for comic books, Chaykin tacitly acknowledges his own complicity in consumer culture. *American Flagg!* thus implied there was hope that individuals in a consumer age could still find room for personal expression by appropriating lowbrow castoffs of American culture."[42] Through this argument, Wright begins to develop an idea of how a commercially successful series might continue to have an outlaw's subversive potential. There is some hope for a post-industrial culture overrun by media, but that hope is not in the culturally approved heights of civilization. It would certainly please Chaykin, a self-proclaimed liberal writing during the Reagan era, to know that his subversive message of hope would be found with Reuben Flagg, a liberal actor turned cynical patriot.

The Shadow of the City: Howard Chaykin's *The Shadow* and *Time2*

As Rose notes in the first favorable mainstream review of *American Flagg!*, Chaykin, at the time, had already largely moved away from full artistic responsibility for the series (first as illustrator and then as writer). His focus then shifted to one project more mainstream (DC's revamp of *The Shadow*) and one less (First's graphic novel presentation of Chaykin's *Time2*); however, both moved Chaykin even further toward the content and themes of traditional crime fiction. In Chaykin's own words, "I've outgrown science fiction… [W]hat I read for relaxation and entertainment is crime fiction… Crime fiction deals with the better stuff, with the more familiar, darker aspects of human greed, and I'm more interested in human greed than galaxy-spanning adventure."[43] Of course, Chaykin couldn't hope for anything more closely associated with crime fiction of the pulps than the character of the Shadow. However, the traditional version of the Shadow presents a vigilante with an absolutist, near-fascist sense of moral authority that seems to work in contrast to the political ideology developed in *American Flagg!*

In many ways, this moral authority became a target in Chaykin's retelling of the Shadow as a modern crime-fighter: "I believe I'm doing some sort of myth-debunking in my reinterpretation of the Shadow."[44] This is accomplished not by rewriting the fictional history of the character but by taking all previous versions of the character's history into account: from the starting point in the 1930s, with Walter B. Gibson portraying the Shadow as a mysteriously trained menace to criminals, to the Cold War variation with Dennis Lynd's rendering of the Shadow as an establishment protector who fought spies.

Fig. 2.6
Margo's age as well as her rebuff take the Shadow, a noir hero, outside his conventional context *The Shadow* No. 3, DC, 1986; The Shadow is the copyright and trademark of Conde Nast. Used with permission.

In a mini-series collected as *The Shadow: Blood and Judgment* (1987), now-aged former agents of the Shadow are systematically killed in brutal ways that pushed the boundaries of the more conservative DC Comics (even with the series marketed exclusively to comic book stores). After a red herring appearance of an elderly man claiming to be the Shadow, Kent Allard reappears in this 1980 timeframe, looking no older than he had before his disappearance some thirty years before. Using the idea that the Shadow had learned his art of deception during his travels in the East, Chaykin reveals the long history of Allard, who in the 1920s accidentally discovered the mystical city of Shambala with the famous heir Lamont Cranston. After killing Cranston to prevent his intended exploitation and destruction of Shambala, Allard learns the secrets of this hidden civilization. Returning to the known world having acquired near-mystical abilities (to extend his life, among other things), Allard assumes the alias of Lamont Cranston and mercilessly fights crime as the Shadow. When Shambala closes its borders in response to the Cold War, Allard retreats from the known world until his agents are murdered.

Chaykin's set-up for this modern tale of the Shadow reconfigures the story in important ways that honor the pulps but also exposes what he considers to be the absurdist nostalgia for a brutal fascist. On one hand, readers accustomed to the more violent action characters of the comic book's direct market can enjoy the images of the Shadow tearing apart criminals with Uzis. On the other hand, the Shadow may still look like a young man, but his story suggests his approach is based on the reactionary politics of a bygone period. All of his agents are now elderly, and the nefarious villain is the original Lamont Cranston, still alive and head of a criminal empire but impotent and wheelchair bound. With a genetically engineered "son," Cranston vainly hoped to transplant his brain into the younger form. More significantly, Allard has a clearly demeaning attitude toward the Shambalan mother of his racially other sons; he is ultimately portrayed as both sexist and racist. Margo Lane, the most famous of the Shadow's agents and his romantic interest, describes him not only as a sexist but also as a cruel and selfish pragmatist: "[You're] a pig–without the "male chauvinist" qualifications… You're a vampire who sucked me into your circle of death–used me for sex–constantly put my life in danger–then left me flat, without a word."[45]

LOOK HERE, MARGO-- I'VE TRIED TO EXPLAIN--
--I HAD NO CHOICE BUT TO LEAVE YOU IN '49--
I'D MADE YOU NO PLEDGES-- NO COMMIT--
"BULL."
YOU'RE A--A VAMPIRE WHO SUCKED ME INTO YOUR CIRCLE OF DEATH--
--USED ME FOR SEX--
--CONSTANTLY PUT MY LIFE IN DANGER--
--THEN LEFT ME FLAT, WITHOUT A WORD--
MARGO-- I'VE--
AND FURTHERMORE--
--ALL THIS SHAMBALA CRAP--
--YOU'VE BEEN LYING TO ME SINCE THE DAY WE MET--
A WAVE OF BRUTAL MURDERS, NATION-WIDE--
--FIRST YOU'RE CRANSTON-- THEN YOU'RE ALLARD--
--WHICH POLICE HAVE DUBBED--
--THE SENIOR CITIZEN SLAYINGS--
--YOU'RE HIDING OUT IN THE ANDES-- THEN IT'S THE HIMALAYAS--
--HOW LONG AM I SUPPOSED TO--:SOB:--
HAVE STRUCK HOME IN A BIZARRE FASHION--
MARGO-- I'M SORRY--
BUT ALL OF US ARE IN GRAVE DANGER--
--OUR BILLY DIAZ SPOKE--
OF WHAT-- DYING?
I'M AN OLD WOMAN, DAMNIT-- I--
--TO RETIRED POLICE INSPECTOR JOSEPH CARDONA
JOE CARDONA?!

And Cranston's trophy wife turns out to be an excessive parody of the femme fatal, extending the caricature of woman like Gabrielle in *Kiss Me Deadly*; she indicates her intention of launching a nuclear device to the Shadow with these words: "Only one other thing got me as hot as you–[and that] was a movie about Hiroshima."[46]
From the excessive level of Allard's sexism to Cranston's trophy wife's selfish and nearly absurd desire leading to widespread destruction, *The Shadow* provides a much more convincing critique of problematic portrayals of women in noir than *American Flagg!*

In addition, the modern media tracked the story of the murders of the former agents of the Shadow, and this led to a new generation of fans for the Shadow (on news programs, it was referred to as "Shadowmania"). Even as Chaykin demonstrated the way the morally questionable anti-heroes of a repressive past became the celebrity heroes of a media age, many reacted with frustration over the way he critiqued an icon of pulp fiction. "Harlan Ellison called Chaykin's Shadow 'vile and detestable' and bemoaned DC's attempt to rein in 'auteurs like him' who were 'mucking with legends.'"[47] Perhaps more interesting is that many more readers disregarded the satire, enthusiastically reading an ongoing series that immediately followed Chaykin's limited series; written by Andy Helfer, the ongoing Shadow series told more stories of the Shadow in a modern setting but in a tone that was much more reverent of the original novels, radio shows, and magazines.

However, Chaykin's treatment of the Shadow shouldn't be read as a rejection of crime fiction but rather a demonstration of his preference for a certain type of crime fiction: "I like [James] Cain. I think Cain creates a very positive, very moralistic world... Cain's are dark novels, but they're human frailty novels... The EC crime books were basically pastiches of Cain with a whiff of Woolrich, about two married people who couldn't stand each other. I found that kind of fascinating."[48] Rather than present a story in the adventure vein typical of American comic books, Chaykin became more interested in a story like those of EC crime books that eschewed heroism and characters that might serve as positive moral guides. The result of this interest would be *Time2: The Epiphany*, the other work from Chaykin published in 1986, but coming from First Comics in a European-style graphic novel format with far fewer mainstream commercial aspirations. Inspired by Phillip K. Dick[49] whose alternative history fiction Chaykin considered not quite science fiction, *Time2* is like *Mister X* as a study of city life but in a way less tied to the plot and more tied to the design. And *Time2* is, like *American Flagg!*, a fully conceived alternative world but in a way less futuristic and more a vision of what New York might have been had World's Fair dreams become nightmares.

Unlike the more broad-based satire of *American Flagg!*, this series portrays the city as less clearly threatening with less centralized oppressive power. In fact, the city offers excitement in the form of licit and illicit entertainments: a new jazz era with nightclubs lining the streets. The menace is more implicit with nothing really for a hero to oppose but much to dread. In a city overrun by neon signs that blend everything sacred and profane, the denizens long for eternal youth and find it in one of two options for life beyond death: Deja-Voodoo (making the buyer into an undead zombie) and Reincarnimation (transferring the buyer's memories into a robotic copy of the buyer). As crime comics writer Jamie S. Rich describes *Time2*, "It's a mash-up of art deco-design, the seediness of old-school New York, and a cynicism about the idea of a better tomorrow."[50] With less of a stress on the encroachment of media culture and more on the overwhelming complexity of city life, Chaykin renders the city as confusing as it is thrilling and potentially as dehumanizing as the options available for life beyond death. *Time2: The Epiphany* begins with the ultimate anxiety of industrial and post-industrial culture: the free-floating threat of the serial killer. Targeting robot (devoidoid) prostitutes, "Mr. Fix-It" is introduced to the readers through a Walter Winchell-type broadcast, literally set atop Mr. Fix-It as he follows and attacks his latest victim. In addition to the text of the broadcast, the panels are further broken up by different modes of graphic experience: the text of billboards and news tickers, textually rendered sound effects, and the credits of the graphic novel (all competing for the reader's attention and in part, obscuring the violent act).

The main plot follows with the report of the death of famous saxophonist and club owner Cosmo Jacobi who supposedly entered into a suicide pact with his mechanical lover. Despite the fact that many suspect something even more seedy, few, including the sinister Chief Inspector Bon Ton MacHoot, care enough to push too hard. Jacobi's wife, Shalimar, hides her joy over his passing from no one, and she is further defined when Ingo, the club emcee, declares to her, "For want of you… I bloodied these hands."[51] She responds with tough, double-edged verbiage that would create envy in almost any fast-talking hard-boiled detective: "Wise up bab–You're a two-bit grifter in a four dollar world… You've got moist hands and a weak mouth–That's two strikes against you already–You slaver when you kiss–Euuuuhhhhh! And you come–like a good dog–when I call… so surely–mutual respect is out of the question."[52] Jacobi's death brings back to town his best friend, Maxim Glory, who left Time2 and his girlfriend, Pansy Matthias, six years ago when he found himself in trouble with local gangsters.

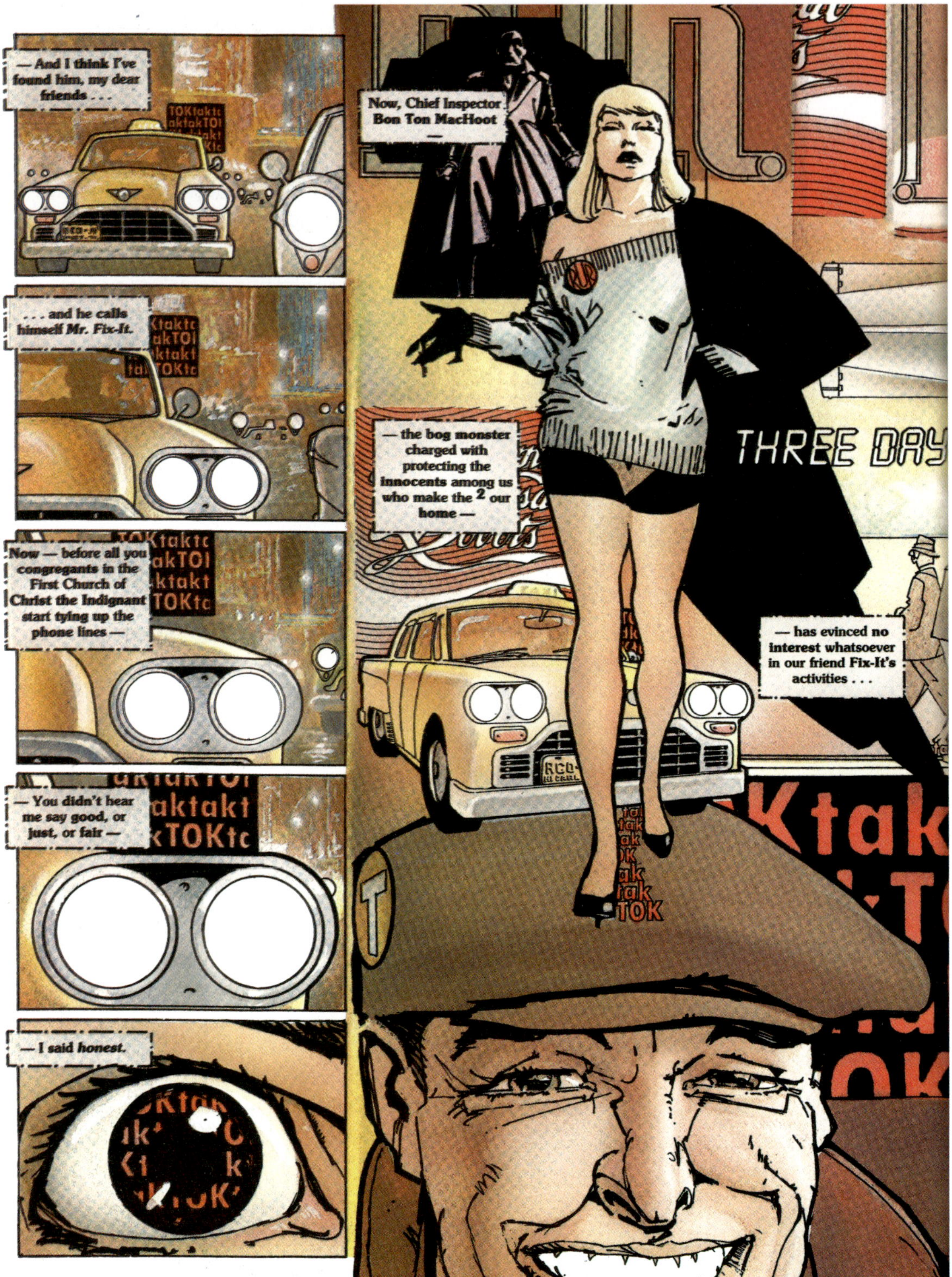
— And I think I've found him, my dear friends . . .
. . . and he calls himself *Mr. Fix-It.*
Now — before all you congregants in the First Church of Christ the Indignant start tying up the phone lines —
— You didn't hear me say good, or just, or fair —
— I said *honest.*
Now, Chief Inspector Bon Ton MacHoot —
— the bog monster charged with protecting the innocents among us who make the 2 our home —
— has evinced no interest whatsoever in our friend Fix-It's activities . . .
THREE DAY

Of course, Glory wants to exact revenge on Jacobi's killer but Chaykin takes "a pretty straight-up potboilin' film noir [revenge] plot"[53] and makes it anything but straight-up. After Glory attacks Ingo, the bloodied and disoriented Ingo runs away, encountering Mr. Fix-It with a special devoidoid sent to find and kill the bad-for-business serial killer. Ingo interrupts Mr. Fix-It's attack on the devoidoid because the prostitute resembles Shalomar. Shifting her attention from Mr. Fix-It to Ingo, the homicidal devoidoid turns his momentary sexual pleasure with her into a horrifyingly violent death. And in the end, Jacobi returns as a robotic version of himself who doesn't believe that his wife had anything to do with his death (even though she is mortified by his return).

Fig. 2.7
The text of city life from the news broadcast to the signage to the credits of the graphic novel itself competes for our attention on the serial killer
Time2: The Epiphany, First, 1986
© Howard Chaykin

This carefully constructed resolution depicts Ingo and Shalimar as suffering but not as a direct result of their crimes. Unlike EC crime comics characters whose sins were always their own undoing, everything in *Time2* seems to point in the wrong direction with the norm being incomplete fulfillment, broken relationships, and malicious desire. And the free-floating threat of Mr. Fix-It is still at large; originally subtitled "Sordid Tales of Vulgar Enlightenment,"[54] *Time2* is described by Chaykin as "an existential crime booking in which nobody gives a fuck who did it."[55] Of course, this description puts the story at odds with the goal of mystery fiction as defined by its historical starting point, the historical era best known as the Enlightenment. Filled with existential dread that rivals and goes beyond that of Cain novels and EC crime comics, the Time2 story continued in 1987 in another graphic novel (*Time2: The Satisfaction of Black Mariah*) further exploring anxieties about the city and its technology. With robots agitating for citizenship and taking shape as uncontrollable threats, Chaykin comically prevents a release from the unrelenting pressure of the city through a very obvious means; Glory is constantly distracted by life in the big city and puts off sex with Matthias, his all-too-willing, somewhat good-girl girlfriend.

Although one of Chaykin's greatest accomplishments in comic book design and crime fiction redesign, *Time2*'s episodic, scatological, and jazz-like plotting failed to excite popular interest in the same way that *American Flagg!* and *The Shadow* had. With First expressing less interest than initially in continuing a series of *Time2* graphic novels, Chaykin had no real outlet for his more adult-oriented material (adult both in terms of graphic content and artistic sophistication); the corporate restrictions placed on him by DC (with whom he would also revamp *Blackhawk* in 1987) would eventually become the focus of his frustrations. Even though DC had become less tied to the Comics Code with their direct-market-only publications, it continued to uphold the standards more than its new upstart competitors.

Due to the violence and sexual references in both *The Shadow* and *Blackhawk*, DC began discussing the use of a rating system to label such direct market publications. Like Alan Moore, Frank Miller, and other star creators of the 1980s who worked with mainstream comic book publishers, Chaykin reacted angrily, seeing it as yet another attempt to limit his creative freedom. "I think the real intention of the ratings system was to put us [creators] in our places."[56]

The Horror of the Industry: Howard Chaykin's Black Kiss

Chaykin's most direct reaction to this perceived bullying could be seen in 1988 with another genre blending comic noir entitled *Black Kiss*. A limited series published by Vortex, *Black Kiss* brought together crime and horror fiction with content designed to intentionally and excessively violate standards of decency that prohibited the use of profanity, portrayals of violence, and the depiction of sex acts. In fact, the content was so controversial that the printer initially refused to produce it, and *Black Kiss* was sent only to direct market stores in plastic bags that prevented casual browsing. In this case, Chaykin seems to have changed the focus of his moral battle as now he had a fight with industry-based prohibitions, taking an outlaw position in order to challenge industry standards.

Black Kiss begins in modern day Los Angles with a transsexual prostitute, Dagmar Laine, and her lover, Beverly Grove, trying to retrieve a film reel from a lecherous priest connected to the Vatican. Eventually, these manipulative femmes fatale seduce and draw into their schemes Cass Pollack, a man on the run from the mob, who the police think is responsible for the murders of his wife and daughter (who were actually killed by the mob). In short order, Pollack realizes that many people want the film reel, including the so-called "Order of Boniface," vampire groupies who know the reel to be a 1920s pornographic film starring "Bubba" Keaton (really a vampire) and Beverly Grove (his sire). Pollack has other revelations, most notably the fact that Laine (altered by surgery to look much like Grove) still possesses a penis. As Laine and Grove leave sex and death in their wake, corrupt police, wronged by Laine and Grove, find Laine and a physically bound Pollack. After the police rape Laine, Grove discovers them and kills them, but a freed Pollack then manages to kill them both.

The rendering of the series in black and white does little to reduce the shock value of the violence and sex, but it certainly creates an atmosphere that is reminiscent of classic film noir, and the blending of crime and horror is reminiscent of the line walked by *Shock SuspenStories*. One of the most controversial scenes is the explicit depiction of Laine's rape by the police, something she afterwards claims to have enjoyed. In some ways, the criticisms of the depiction of women in *American Flagg!* have the potential to make more disturbing Chaykin's portrayal of Grove as the ultimate femme fatale and Laine as a femme fatale/transsexual who enjoys rape. However, the blending of crime and horror makes them into vampire and minion and suggests that Chaykin is exploring the nature of crime stereotypes by pushing them to a breaking point. After all, the male protagonists of crime fiction often fall into the web of women who understand their very male needs too well, and *Black Kiss* points out the person best able to do that might be someone formerly or partially male: an implication that serves as a radical exposure of the psychology of crime fiction.[57] It wouldn't be difficult to for some to define the profanity, violence, and sex as gratuitous, but such a definition seems to be beside the point of *Black Kiss*.

In order to challenge the standards set by the industry, Chaykin presents almost everything that Wertham feared in comic books and more. Whether or not readers agree with his particular approach in *Black Kiss*, Chaykin is intent on challenging the belief that a system is good just because it identifies itself as good. In reference to his refusal to live up to expectations for the American comic book that is focused on heroes, Chaykin makes this statement about *Black Kiss*: "Comic book characters, generally speaking are paradigms. I'm not interested in doing cut and dry heroic adventure stories."[58] Inarguably, he does much more than create weak heroes or antiheroes in his work, but that is an important facet of his work. With their genre blending works, both Motter and Chaykin guard against a potential pitfall of challenging the standards set by the industry; they never present their protagonists as completely viable, heroic alternatives to the current system. By blending crime fiction with science fiction (and horror fiction), Motter and Chaykin reconsidered and revitalized crime fiction in the midst of the new phenomenon of direct market comic books. However, it was Frank Miller, with his blending of crime fiction and superhero fiction, who would create the real resurgence of crime comics in the mainstream market, eventually inaugurating a raw, unblended form of comic noir with *Sin City*.

Chapter 2 Notes

1 Bradford W. Wright, *Comic Book Nation: The Transformation of Youth Culture in America* (Baltimore: Johns Hopkins University Press, 2001), 181.

2 Randy Duncan and Matthew Smith, *The Power of Comics: History, Form, and Culture* (New York: Continuum, 2009), 41–42.

3 Jean-Paul Gabilliet, *Of Comics and Men: A Cultural History of American Comic Books*, trans. Bart Beatty and Nick Nguyen (Jackson: University of Mississippi Press, 2010), 45.

4 Duncan and Smith, *The Power of Comics*, 58.

5 Gabilliet, *Of Comics and Men*, 86–87.

6 Of course, the term independent should be understood as being relative, ranging from self-publishers to new (albeit smaller) corporate publishers; both types were enabled by new, cheaper printing technology and the direct market.

7 James Ursini, "Noir Science," *Film Noir Reader* 2, ed. Alain Silver and James Ursini (New York: Limelight Editions, 1999), 231–233.

8 Woody Haut, *Neon Noir: Contemporary American Crime Fiction* (London: Serpent's Tail, 1999), 180.

9 Ibid., 181.

10 Ralph Willett, *The Naked City: Urban Crime Fiction in the USA* (Manchester: Manchester University Press, 1996), 4.

11 Ibid., 18.

12 Jeffrey Klaehn, "Mister M: A Career Retrospective with Dean Motter," *Graphic Novel Reporter*, last modified June 25, 2011, http://graphicnovelreporter.com/content/mister-m-career-retrospective-dean-motter-interview.

13 Anthony Vidler, *The Architectural Uncanny: Essays in Modern Unhomely* (Cambridge: MIT, 1992), ix.

14 Arlen Schumer, "Introduction," *Mister X: The Definitive Collection*, Vol. 1, by Dean Motter (New York: Simon and Schuster, 2004), 13.

15 Howard Chaykin, "Introduction," *Mister X: Condemned*, by Dean Motter (Milwaukie, OR: Dark Horse, 2009), 7.

16 Dean Motter, *Mister X: The Definitive Collection*, Vol. 1 (New York: Simon and Schuster, 2004), 47.

17 Henry Jenkins, "The Future Isn't What It Used to Be: An Interview with Comics Creator Dean Motter," *Confessions of an Aca-Fan*, last modified June 6, 2007, http://henryjenkins.org/2007/06/an_interview_with_comics_creat.html.

18 Ibid.

19 Motter, *Mister X: The Definitive Collection*, Vol. 1, 70.

20 Jenkins, "The Future Isn't What It Used to Be."

21 Henry Jenkins, "'The Tomorrow That Never Was'—Retrofuturism in the Comics of Dean Motter," *Comics and the City: Urban Space in Print, Picture, and Sequence*, ed. Jorn Ahrens and Arno Meteling (New York: Continuum, 2010), 82.

22 Ibid., 64.

23 Ibid., 75.

24 Willett, *The Naked City,* 2.

25 Dean Motter, *Mister X: The Definitive Collection*, Vol. 2 (New York: Simon and Schuster, 2005), 202.

26 Jeffrey Morgan, "Motivation by Obsession: The Architect and the Archetype." *Mister X: The Definitive Collection*, Vol. 2, by Dean Motter (New York: Simon and Schuster, 2005), 6.

27 Michael Morcock, "Introduction," *American Flagg!: Hard Times*, by Howard Chaykin (Evanston, IL: First Comics 1985), 2.

28 Jorn Ahrens and Arno Meteling, *Comics and the City: Urban Space in Print, Picture, and Sequence* (New York: Continuum, 2010), 6.

29 *Dreadstar* was first published by Marvel's Epic imprint.

30 Brannon Costello, *Howard Chaykin: Conversations* (Jackson: University Press of Mississippi, 2011), 180.

31 Ibid., 173.

32 Howard Chaykin, *American Flagg!* (Berkley, CA: Image Comics, 2008), 99.

33 Ibid., 215.

34 Ibid., 216.

35 Brannon Costello, *Howard Chaykin: Conversations*, 109.

36 Ibid., 62–63.

37 Benjamin Demott, "Darkness at the Mall: The 'New Wave' in Adult Comic Books Features Defeat, Cynicism, and Despair," *Psychology Today*, February 1984, 48.

38 Ibid., 51–52.

39 Ibid., 52.

40 Rose, Lloyd, "Comics Books for Grown-Ups," *The Atlantic Monthly*, August 1986, 80.

41 Ibid., 80.

42 Wright, *Comic Book Nation*, 269.

43 Gary Groth and Robert Fiore, *The New Comics: Interviews from the Pages of The Comics Journal* (New York: Berkley, 1988), 88.

44 Ibid., 86.

45 Howard Chaykin, *The Shadow: Blood and Judgment* (New York: DC Comics, 1987), 72.

46 Ibid., 124.

47 Costello, *Howard Chaykin: Conversations*, 79.

48 Ibid., 221.

49 Ibid., 72–73.

50 James S. Rich, "Review: *Time2: The Epiphany; Time2: The Satisfaction of Black Mariah,*" *Trouble with Comics*, last modified December 2010, http://troublewithcomics.com/post/490426056/guest-reviewer-month-jamie-s-rich-on-howard.

51 Howard Chaykin, *Time2: The Epiphany* (Evanston, IL: First Comics, 1986), 21.

52 Ibid., 22.

53 Rich, "Review: *Time2: The Epiphany; Time2: The Satisfaction of Black Mariah.*"

54 Costello, Brannon, *Howard Chaykin: Conversations*, 133.

55 Groth and Fiore, *The New Comics*, 93.

56 Costello, *Howard Chaykin: Conversations*, 99.

57 *Black Kiss* (1988) predates *The Crying Game* (1992), a neo-noir film with a similar transsexual revelation scene and a similar commentary on film noir.

58 Costello, *Howard Chaykin: Conversations*, 126.

NO!
YOU'LL KILL NO ONE
--EV AGA
YOU WO T SAVE M NOT LIK BEFOR

CHAPTER 3

The Dark Night Returns to the Mainstream: Frank Miller

The noir hero is a knight in blood caked armor. He's dirty and he does his best to deny the fact that he's a hero the whole time.
Frank Miller[1]

Superheroes and Vigilantes: Frank Miller's Classic Criminal

For many reasons, the superhero story dominated the comics industry in the Comics Code era and continued to be the dominant genre in the direct market and mainstream comic book business. This continued dominance had much to do with the genre's flexibility or at least the perception of its flexibility by the industry (DC and later Marvel) and the consumer. Although superheroes like Superman and Batman were originally vigilantes who worked outside the laws of an unjust system, their patriotic makeover during World War II demonstrated that they could be readily reshaped to better suit popular demand. Consequently, DC redesigned its superhero properties in the 1950s to more exclusively target a youth audience and live up to the standards of the Comics Code. As previously mentioned, one of the ironies in the relative success of Fredric Wertham's campaign against crime comics is that superhero comics, one of his ancillary targets, became the new force to support conventional authority in the Comics Code era. Despite being labeled by Wertham as crime stories, the superhero stories of the 1950s became anything but an exploration of the desperation and anxieties of industrial and post-industrial life. "DC aligned its superheroes squarely on the side of established authority, with it naturally equated with the best interests of American citizens… DC's comic books emphasized responsibility to the community over individualism."[2] The science fiction superhero Superman became the big blue Boy Scout most people now know him to be, and the noir superhero Batman "fared much worse."[3] Forsaking his premise in a more dramatic way, Batman became escapist as well as establishment-approving with fantastic plots involving magic and aliens from outer space.

Marvel soon became a force to rival DC's dominance in the market by presenting itself as more of the same but with a distinct twist that appealed to older, less conservative readers. With the Fantastic Four, the Hulk, and Spider-Man, Marvel grounded their adventures more in the real world and "began to turn out flawed heroes one after another."[4] At the forefront was Spider-Man, a self-conscious treatment of the superhero that worked against conventions. Peter Parker was the intellectual high school misfit (a stereotype of the superhero comic book reader), and he would initially use his superpowers for personal gain, questioning the trope that superpowers naturally led to costumed crime fighting. Due to Peter's reckless behavior, his Uncle Ben was killed, and the darker emotion of guilt would motivate him (much as revenge motivated Batman). Thereafter, "[t]he young, flawed, and brooding antihero became the most widely imitated archetype in the superhero genre since the appearance of Superman."[5] In years to come, *Spider-Man* was published without Comics Code approval in order to present an anti-drug story of Harry Osborn's drug addiction.[6] More poignantly but less controversially, when the Green Goblin kills Spider-Man's girlfriend, Peter Parker chooses not to care for Harry, his ailing friend, in order to seek revenge against the Green Goblin. As might be expected, this drug story fell far short of the seedy drama of "The Monkey" in *Shock SuspenStories* decades earlier, and Peter Parker never turned into a crime story antihero, with no serious consequences resulting from Spider-Man's revenge story; Harry ultimately recovered and the Green Goblin was killed by his own glider.

Even though the growing popularity of Marvel comics caused DC to become more realistic and less clearly endeared to all authority in the 1970s, Marvel's and DC's new vision of superheroes still posed far from a forthright challenge to the system. This may be best represented by the first comic book that Marvel used as its entrée into the direct market in 1981–*Dazzler*, featuring a sexy, disco-themed superheroine developed cross-promotionally with Casablanca Records. Regardless, once the transition to the direct market was made in the early 1980s, DC and Marvel continued to dominate and flourish, with their basic superhero tropes influencing countless independent publishers. Despite Dean Motter's and Howard Chaykin's relative success and influence on creators, neither caused publishers to make a major turn away from the superhero story. With no obvious end to the reign of the superhero in sight, it would be hard to imagine the full-fledged reemergence of crime comics without a creator who captured the popular interests of superhero comic book readers in the 1980s.

The one creator most responsible for blending superhero and crime stories and eventually paving the way for a more orthodox crime comic was Frank Miller. In love with the medium but strangely unprepared to illustrate superhero comic books, Frank Miller came from Vermont to New York with a portfolio that included illustrations of classic type characters from hard-boiled detective novels:

> [B]ack when I was an amateur, and through to this day, the bulk of my fiction writing has been old crime novels… The crime fiction from the 1940s and '50s remains my favorite, the era that, in many ways, Dashiell Hammett started and Chandler refined, along with Jim Thompson, James M. Cain, Charles Willeford, and Spillane. So as an amateur, the comics I did generally were crime stories: tough guys in trench coats and spooky urban landscapes.[7]

With the rise in popularity in the late 1970s seen with new crime novelists like Elmore Leonard and neo-noir directors like Brian DePalma, it may have seemed like a good time for such material. However, Miller was much more interested in classic crime, and almost every publisher told him superhero comics were the only game in the comic book industry.

Blind and in the Dark: Frank Miller's *Daredevil*

Nevertheless, with superhero comic books as a point of inspiration for him as an illustrator in his youth,[8] Miller adapted to the needs of the industry in the late 1970s. In particular, he refined his craft with advice from Neal Adams, who had worked for both of the big two and was a fan favorite for his work on *Batman* with writer Denny O'Neil. In an effort to return Batman to his crime story roots, O'Neil and Adams made Gotham City into a dark and nefarious haven for criminals, with long shadows and stylized presentations of the long-caped Batman emerging from those shadows. However, more than anything else, Adams was known for his intricate line-work, realistic shadows, complex depth of scene, and in-depth research of interior and exterior urban spaces. In an early interview with *The Comics Journal*, Miller suggests that this may have been the most important lesson he learned from Adams: "Neal taught me to check my facts before I started drawing. He said that many times."[9] Miller tried initially to depict this type of realism in his work as a filler artist and on a six-issue stint on *The Spectacular Spider-Man*, but his style would be refined during his work on *Daredevil*, retaining a sense of realism while becoming darker and more stylized. Miller acknowledged a debt to Will Eisner and made a crucial connection between the look of noir fiction and the psychologically distorted world of German expressionism: "I've been watching some German Expressionist movies, and I've found the way that they create sets just for psychological purposes is something comic book artists could do a hell of a lot more... I see the ways that Eisner brought Expressionism into his work–stairwells that were 50 feet long, ceilings that were 100 feet high."[10]

Beginning as co-plotter and illustrator for *Daredevil*, Miller expressed an interest in writing and in short order was allowed to write and illustrate *Daredevil*, a title perennially low-ranking in sales. After taking over the narrative reins of the underperforming title, Miller expressed his admiration for Wally Wood's work on *Daredevil* in the 1960s,[11] but at that time, *Daredevil* was not much of a crime comic (despite the EC crime comic associations that Wood's name might have).[12] Nevertheless, *Daredevil* was a good starting point for Miller in the superhero industry considering Marvel's devotion to the real-world city of New York and Daredevil's limited powers as a superhero. These factors gave Miller the opportunity to explore the nature of city life and make a superhero story more into the crime story that Wertham feared it was.

While almost all superheroes have traumatic origins, Daredevil was created as a handicapped superhero whose disability was an essential part of his superheroism. Matt Murdock lost his sight in an accident that exaggerated all of his other senses, and his "radar sense" allowed him to be a super-acrobat who fought crime. Even before Miller became *Daredevil*'s full-time writer, Daredevil had developed a darker backstory that allowed Miller to explore the conflicted protagonist at the center of crime fiction, torn between social expectations and personal desires. Murdock was a lawyer by day and vigilante by night, and he had become a lawyer at his father's insistence, hoping his son might become a force for good who didn't fight the world with his fists. However, Murdock's father was Jack "Daredevil" Murdock, a small-time boxer who was connected to organized crime.

Miller contributed rather substantially to the series' identity as a crime story with his increasingly stylized visuals and with a rather substantial addition to Murdock's backstory. In his college years, Murdock fell in love with Elektra Natchois, whose father's death would drive her to violence; years later, once Murdock had assumed the identity of Daredevil, she would return as an assassin, highly trained in martial arts and often aligned with forces set against Daredevil. Miller explains, "I ripped off the first Sand Saref story [in *The Spirit*] to do the first Elektra story. Rather than just regurgitating it, though, I put a harsher edge on the conflict. I had there be more consequences to the fact that he was living with a contradiction in that he loved a woman and she was his enemy."[13]

With Elektra developed less as a character and more as an open space within Murdock's psyche, Murdock is metaphorically blind to her faults and Elektra becomes Daredevil's femme fatale—and tragic love—eventually killed by a rival assassin named Bullseye. Like other women in crime fiction, Elektra is the problematic unknown, emblematic of Matt Murdoch's desires that are unfulfilled not only by his work as a lawyer (bound by socially imposed rules) but also by his fight as a vigilante (bound by self-imposed rules).

Other elements of crime fiction character types also make their way into Miller's first run on the series, such as the chain-smoking everyman reporter Ben Urich, someone who wants to fight the system from the inside but finds it nearly impossible. More important is Miller's makeover of the Spider-Man villain known as the Kingpin, a formerly orange-vested, purple-panted caricature of a big crime boss. In addition to transforming him into a genuine crime boss protected by the law and corrupting the city, Miller humanizes Kingpin as Wilson Fisk. Before he returns as the villain in *Daredevil*, Fisk is presented as a retired crime boss, desperately in love with his wife, who understands his past but has convinced him to live differently. Only when she is killed by his former enemies does Fisk return to exact his revenge and become the untouchable crime boss of New York City. In a continued effort to make unclear the line between heroism and villainy in a system that privileges the powerful, Daredevil becomes a hero whose methods of intimidation and violence are no longer clearly separated from those of the criminals.

In the issue in which Elektra is killed, Miller demonstrates his mastery of the medium by skillfully drawing out her execution at the hands of the costumed killer Bullseye (and thereby pushing the boundaries of the Comics Code in one of its safest genres). In addition to dramatically emphasizing her stabbing, Miller uses a series of smaller panels to show the dying Elektra crawling to Murdock's home set against backgrounds of a city filled with bystanders who don't care. And in a way that undermines standard expectations of the superhero, Daredevil defeats Bullseye and saves him from falling to his death but then rethinks the situation and lets him fall. Bullseye: "No! You won't save me—not like before! Kill you! I'll kill—" Daredevil: "You'll kill no one—ever again."[14] In short order, Daredevil has made a transition from Stan Lee's platitude-spouting, left-of-center bleeding heart to a tough (albeit conflicted) crime story protagonist.

NO!
YOU WON'T SAVE ME-- NOT LIKE BEFORE!
KILL YOU! I'LL KILL--
YOU'LL KILL NO ONE--
--EVER AGAIN!

Fig. 3.1
Daredevil decides not to save Bullseye and Daredevil more clearly becomes a noir superhero
Daredevil No. 181, Marvel, 1982 © Marvel

Throughout Miller's run on *Daredevil*, one of Miller's innovations is the gradual loss of the heavy-handed, omniscient, and moralistic voice of the comic book narrator associated with Stan Lee and Marvel comics. In "Roulette," the final issue in his first run on the series, in a way similar to the main character's narration of a hard-boiled detective novel or a voice-over in film noir, the narrator is Daredevil himself. After a tragic shooting causes Murdock to "see" how others respect his violence and not his moral authority, Daredevil visits the hospital bedside of a completely paralyzed Bullseye. In panels that serve to fracture the typically unified self of the superhero, Daredevil's loss of a sense of self drives him to a game of Russian roulette with Bullseye. As he reflects on his life, Daredevil's voice is unreliable as a moral center; he is unable to recognize the problematic connection between the violence and the morality taught to him by his boxer father. Perhaps even worse in the end is the revelation that the gun contained no bullets, the whole incident taking shape as a means to maliciously taunt his now-helpless enemy. And in a way that further deconstructs the superhero through the use of crime story conventions, Miller returned to the series for a six-issue run referred to as *Daredevil: Born Again*. The series was a collaboration between Miller as writer and David Mazzucchelli as illustrator, whose style walks a line between the realism and stylization of film noir. Plucking Karen Page, the relatively innocent former girlfriend to Daredevil, out of the Silver Age starting point of the series, Miller transforms her into a junkie who will sell her body and Daredevil's true identity for a fix. Eventually, the information makes its way to the Kingpin, and he systematically destroys Murdock's life, leaving Murdock paranoid, delusional, and homeless. The superhero power fantasy is undermined by having Daredevil's direct physical confrontation with the Kingpin end in easy defeat. And in the end, the Kingpin's assassin (borrowed from a black ops government program) can only be stopped with the help of the super-team, the Avengers (and a subsequently disillusioned Captain America).

Through his blending of the superhero story with the crime story, Miller replaces the optimistic view of the modern civilization (seen in most Comics Code superhero comic books) with Daredevil's unsuccessful attempts to break free of widespread corruption. In traditional noir fashion but in a way that deconstructs the superhero, Daredevil unfairly idealizes the seductive woman, and the paranoid perspective of the male hero becomes apparent to the reader but not necessarily to the hero. The shock value of this work was also recognized by critics who were able to put it into an appropriate framework; in *Dark Knights: The New Comics in Context*, Greg S. McCue states, "The ambiguities in assigning good and evil became more obvious as the characters engaged in ever more ruthless battles... Miller's comics were hard-boiled."[15] In addition, social and political commentary (always implicitly part of crime comics but missing from superhero comics for decades) was also identified as an essential part of Miller's *Daredevil* work. In "Blind Daring," Tim Blackmore argues, "This backdrop of darkness and despair loom over a few islands of kinship... [Miller's] view of a simple[r] America is not naïve. Miller, suspicious of politics, has made sure that 'strong political themes have run throughout his recent comics work.'"[16] Miller took Daredevil from its extreme low point in sales to its place as one of Marvel's most popular titles with his "work on Daredevil [making] him one of the industry's biggest stars."[17] Due to this popularity, many other superhero creators tried to emulate Miller's style with grim and gritty superheroes and more graphic content but did not understand the artistic basis for his transformation of Daredevil. As a consequence, "[f]ew superhero comic books approached the accomplished sophistication achieved by Frank Miller, Howard Chaykin, and Alan Moore."[18] Nevertheless, the popularity of Miller and his superhero/crime concoction would enable him to remake Batman, a more clearly iconic noir superhero, paving the way for his independence from the big two.

A Gumshoe with a Mask: Frank Miller's *The Dark Knight Returns*

In the relatively short tenure of his initial run on *Daredevil*, Miller became a fan favorite at conventions and a critical darling even with tough anti-superhero voices like *The Comics Journal*. In an industry that tended to revolve around trademarked characters rather comic book creators, Miller understood that readers were now buying *his* work rather than the latest *Daredevil* story, and he would use his superstar status to do something not often seen: move back and forth between the big two. In 1983, Miller produced a limited series for DC entitled *Ronin* in a deluxe format aimed at the direct market (high-quality paper with no advertisements). The series portrayed an ancient demon and his archrival, a renegade samurai, reborn in a cyberpunk-style futuristic setting. Within this ultra-corrupt, totalitarian world, Miller used his Ronin character to explore quintessential noir questions such as how someone (like Philip Marlowe) might retain a personal code against overwhelming pressure. And with illustration influenced by manga such as *Lone Wolf and Cub* and Franco-Belgian comic books such as Moebius's science fiction work, Miller's style accentuated the moody expressionist look as his cityscapes became more abstract and experimental: "Miller's comics... showed that an adult milieu need not be tied to commonplace reality or social relevance to be effective."[19] Miller's continued popularity allowed him to have remarkable creative control over an end-of-career story for Batman, one of DC's most valuable properties. After years of work, *The Dark Knight Returns* was released in 1986 and became a work that furthered Miller's crime comics-influenced revision of superheroics throughout the industry. Amplifying his dark aesthetic in visual and narrative terms, Miller was to rob Gotham of its Technicolor gleam and in a way few fans fully recognized, take away from Batman his unquestioned right to righteous violence.

Beginning with the city and the hero's relationship to it, *The Dark Knight Returns* portrays Gotham City as more crime-ridden since Batman retired ten years earlier upon the death of the second Robin, Jason Todd. At 55, Bruce Wayne walks down garbage-filled streets, bleached of traditional comic book color, and revisits crime alley, where his parents were killed. In his own thoughts, he refers to Batman in the third person: "For a moment, I forget that it's all over... but Batman was a young man. If it was revenge he was after, he's taken it. It's been forty years since he was born... born here... It could be happening now. They could be lying at your feet twitching, bleeding... and the man who stole all sense of your life, he could be standing... right over there."[20] Looking at members of the Mutants (the outlaw gang that has overrun Gotham City) beginning to encircle him, Wayne continues in his thoughts, mistaking the Mutants for the mugger who killed his parents: "It is him, it is, and we know so many ways to hurt him... so many lovely ways to punish him... No, it's not him."[21]

In essence, Miller begins with Wayne in the midst of a prolonged schizoid state, similar to what Daredevil passed through in *Born Again*. With Wayne ground down by the culture of the civilized world, the only release and corrective he once knew is Batman whom he increasingly refers to as an animal fighting to be free. According to Miller, this stylized representation of civilization and the city comes out of his own experience as a city-dweller: "After eight years [in New York], it became clear to me that the normal human response to the crime and unending hostility of the city would be to become as ungentlemanly and uncivilized as the city's customs demand."[22] Miller's words are mirrored in Jesse Nash's critical assessment of *The Dark Knight Returns*, with the rationality of the Enlightenment era understood as false: "Frank Miller's Dark Knight is not comfortable with his schizoid state... the human civilization of Gotham City is a sham; what is required is that one become an animal, a human-becoming-intense. Miller's Dark Knight is such a 'becoming,' a creature no longer under rational control, because rationality as a convention only protects the powerful."[23] The retrofuturistic look of Gotham City makes the landscape one of 1950s but coats it with a post-Comics Code grime that represents the great anxiety of modern crime comics: the pervasive rot of civilization.

When Wayne answers the city's call to again become Batman and fight crime, he is less heroic in stereotypical superheroic terms, enjoying the violent means he uses to stop crime. In several different situations, traditional Batman villains are set up as mirrors of Batman, partners in a continually escalating cycle of violence. With his newly repaired face and his return to crime, Two-Face is seen by Batman as "a reflection"[24] and the Joker awakes from a catatonic state only because he overhears media coverage of Batman back in action. In addition, the city remains dubious in their appreciation of this hero. Miller transforms comic book panels into television screens to depict newsroom talk shows that give equal time to Batman's proponents and detractors. With these panel transitions suggesting reality is tied to media construction, the talk show discussions also suggest that the good and evil rhetoric of traditional superheroes is reaching a point of obsolescence, for better or worse. Miller described his attachment to Batman, seeing him, like Dirty Harry, as "a profoundly, consistently moral force, administering the 'Wrath of God' on murderers who society treats as victims."[25] Within the series, Batman may intentionally inflict pain but does so against more violent criminals, and he upholds his traditional stance against killing. However, despite Miller's proclaimed appreciation for Batman's heroism, *The Dark Knight Returns* casts doubt on Batman's methods and presents a worldview outside that of mainstream America, questioning democracy, capitalism, and America's love of the hero with unlimited power. When he defeats the leader of the Mutants, the remaining members of the criminal gang become "sons of Batman"; in short order, the gang splinters further into the Jokers and the Nixons and it becomes apparent that they admired Batman's power and not his morality.

Although Batman fights his old nemeses Two-Face and the Joker, these lunatic villains are far from the ultimate threats to Batman's world (with Two-Face captured at the end of issue one and the Joker dead by his own means at the end of issue three in a four-issue series); the real problem for Batman is the cultural system that institutionalizes corruption and absolves criminals that operate in the court of public opinion and far beyond any true court. Engaging the real world more discretely and yet broadening his artistic style to include caricature, Miller creates a parody of Bernhard Goetz as a paranoid man who pushes a man on crutches into the path of an oncoming train. In addition to the fat white male politicians in Gotham steam rooms, Miller parodies Ronald Reagan as an overly paternal president who genuinely embraces his simplistic, folksy illusion of the country. The president enters the story when Batman becomes a news sensation and exposes local and national politicians' inability to handle the domestic affairs of Gotham City and beyond. In order to maintain the illusion of American security, the president asks another DC icon, Superman, to talk to Batman. In this often-mentioned conversation in the series, Superman is introduced to the reader through a sequence of panels that shows the American flag morphing into the S-shaped symbol on Superman's chest. However, even though many fans have read Superman as a government stooge within the series, Miller gives Superman a voice, creating potential sympathy for him and his perspective.

> We almost threw a party when you retired... Do you remember why you retired, Bruce? No–just look at you–you'd do it again–and like a murderer, you'd cover it up again. Nothing matters to you–except your holy war... I gave them my obedience and my invisibility. They gave me a license and let us live. No, I don't like it but I get to save lives–and the media stays quiet. But now the storm is growing again–they'll hunt us down again–because of you.[26]

Batman's worldview is limited to Gotham City, and he has the luxury to think in rather idealistic, local terms while Superman's worldview is much larger and forces him into global situations that may necessitate moral compromise and conciliation.

In a way that further opens interpretive space within the work, the narration of the story is not supplied by an omniscient narrator but by a character within the story (like so much of hardboiled detective fiction). However, the narration is not limited to the perspective of just one character–Batman–but as in the above case, the narration is also provided by other characters like Superman, Commissioner Gordon, the new Robin, and even the Joker. Also, Miller employs selective exaggeration to portray Batman as a grotesque to emphasize the questionable nature of his moral decisions to highlight his identity as something other than Bruce Wayne, society's model of success. Regardless, Batman is the noir hero in a noir story that indicts a system that would pit Superman against Batman, flawed though they both might be. A study of the fantasies created by the media and the corruption of power, this work returns to noir themes in complex ways, with Batman hopelessly separated from the powerful, the source of the corruption he fights. Tim Blackmore suggests that *The Dark Knight Returns* addresses a fundamental anxiety of contemporary culture: "As social and bureaucratic structures become vast and incomprehensible to people, they retreat into a world of heroes who live by simple, understandable creeds."[27] In *The Dark Knight Returns*, that simple hero could be the paternalistic Reaganesque president for the country as a whole or it could be Batman for Gotham City.

MY NAME IS
DON

Blackmore refers to Howard Chaykin and his uneasiness with such a situation because it causes people to find perfection in fallible human beings. "Chaykin's discomfort is understandable when we consider what kind of power the charismatic individual will have: he will be unequalled, with a mass society at his bequest."[28] However, even though Miller may consider his Batman to be a noir hero ill-fitted for leadership, he also considers Batman a myth: exposing the shortcomings of civilization and willing to give up his status as a hero of the people. "Miller… desires the formation of collectives, and a widespread rise in personal responsibility, strength, and accountability. He too looks toward a decentralized model in which more local power runs a local world, in which the 'vigilante' and 'rebel leader' are unnecessary."[29] In the end, Batman fakes his own death to sidestep the onslaught of the system and like a militia leader, begins to organize cells to undermine the powers-that-be.

Fig. 3.2
Miller's style becomes more abstract and his renderings of Batman often verge on caricature
The Dark Knight Returns No. 4, DC, 1986;
Batman is the copyright and trademark of DC Comics

The Dark Knight Returns was well received by fans and critics and, along with Alan Moore's *Watchmen*, is generally credited with instigating darker and more nihilistic superhero stories. If one series definitively made superhero comics into crime comics (as Wertham had classified them), it was *The Dark Knight Returns*, a series that used noir ideas to deconstruct the superhero. With this in mind, it's particularly interesting that *The Dark Knight Returns* is the only series mentioned in all of the three most significant mainstream articles from the 1980s based on the startling revelation that comic books were suitable for adults: Lloyd Rose's "Comic Books for Grown Ups" in *The Atlantic* (1986), Peter S. Prescott's "The Comic Book (Gulp!) Grows Up" in *Newsweek* (1988), and Jay Cocks and John E. Gallagher's "The Passing of Pow! And Blam!" in *Time* (1988). Of course, the novelty of a superhero comic book written with an adult audience in mind may have been the factor that earned it a place in all three articles; however, some critics still read it with knee-jerk responses to its content, not as extreme but similar in tone to alarmist screeds of the 1940s and 1950s. "While… ambivalences are central to Batman's character and its tension between nobility and savagery, the wider audience and larger media response to *Dark Knight* seems to have focused on only the violent adult side."[30] For instance, Prescott criticized the series, stating, Miller's "Batman reads like a story board for the Bernhard Goetz School of Social Work."[31] Prescott clearly missed Miller's rather obvious parody of Goetz's vigilantism in *The Dark Knight Returns*. Although simplistic criticisms followed Miller throughout his career, *The Dark Knight Returns* would change perspectives within the superhero industry and allowed Miller to put out more stories that crossed boundaries. In 1987, Miller reteamed with illustrator David Mazzucchelli to produce a new origin story for Batman in *Batman: Year One*.

One of its most interesting features is that the narration of the series is shared in equal degrees by Batman and James Gordon; the young policeman's experience presents a quintessential crime story of corruption and personal fallibility that recalls James Cain, and Gordon's story arguably subsumes that of the superhero. At this point in his career, Miller said, "I'm not interested in superheroes operating in a superhero world."[32]

The Rough Road to Black and White: Interlude

The publication process resulting in *Batman: Year One* led Miller to a literal and ideological departure from the cultural hegemony of the big two. Six months after he had written the series, completely illustrated and lettered, Miller received a call from DC asking him to rewrite six pages that depicted Selina Kyle (the future Catwoman) as a prostitute. Reading this request as DC's preemptive move to ward off the controversy that might accompany the depiction, Miller refused and it went to press as it was originally written.[33] Miller was frustrated by the industry's market driven concerns and need to remain safe within the court of public opinion, understanding such a position to be antithetical to the First Amendment and the development of comic book art. Bitterly, Miller would complain, "As far as I know, the comics industry has never done a fucking thing for the First Amendment."[34] In the late 1980s, Miller wouldn't be alone in his outspoken opinions, thanks to the rise of comic book creators as celebrities within the new comic book culture. Thereby, Alan Moore, Howard Chaykin, Dave Sim, and others had significant power within the increasingly intertwined mainstream and independent comic book publishing worlds; they pushed for creators' rights and advocated finding publishers other than DC and Marvel, publishers who had fewer commercial concerns and less prohibitive control over the creators. When Dave Sim and Scott McCloud produced the "Creator's Bill of Rights" in the 1980s, the movement attracted many different advocates.[35] Dave Sim, creator of *Cerebus*, was idealistic in his belief in artistic freedom and his criticism of company control, while Peter Eastman and Peter Laird, creators of *Teenage Mutant Ninja Turtles*, were pragmatic in their desire to protect creators' abilities to profit from original work. Miller was idealistic, pragmatic, and also extremist in his approach, broadly defining censorship to include even a company's self-regulation of its employees.

Eventually becoming an enthusiastic supporter of Denis Kitchen's Comic Book Legal Defense Fund, established to help protect creators prosecuted for obscenity, etc., Miller traced the problems in the industry back to Fredric Wertham, the Kefauver hearings, and the creation of the Comics Code: "Comics declared themselves completely impotent in the '50s with the Comics Code."[36] In addition, he understood Bill Gaines's generous attitude toward his employees as creators to be foundational to the idea of creators' rights and responsible for producing one of the high points in American comic book history. "EC does represent the most consistently well-crafted line of comics to date… EC is relevant to this conversation because it demonstrated what strong management can do, if management is dedicated to quality."[37] And fundamentally connected to this appreciation of Bill Gaines and the quality of EC crime comics[38] is his belief that industrial and post-industrial models of business work against the individual: "Ironically, [the Comics Code] was created when Bill Gaines called a meeting of publishers to fight censorship. The other publishers wrote it, and enforced it as much as the distributors. They wanted Gaines out."[39] Like Howard Chaykin, Miller understood DC's rating system as a front end attempt to restrict creators[40] and that restriction enabled the evil of dogmatic moralists like Edwin Meese and Jerry Falwell (who targeted comic books as a bad influence): "I believe they have to be fought. I believe any concession to them does no good at all. Tactically, I think it just encourages them, and morally, it's offensive to everything I believe in."[41] In a way that appropriates the tough guy talk of his noir heroes, Miller argued against the personal weakness of continuing to work within the mainstream: "Company loyalty is the battered wife's excuse."[42] Miller decided to begin his fight with social, political, and industry-based prohibitions by becoming something of an outlaw and taking his talent outside the mainstream. Interested in challenging industry standards with distinctly adult comic book art, Miller began working with Dark Horse, one of the independent publishers most fiercely devoted to creators' rights. And he would eventually realize his desire to be free from the big two by embracing crime comics in a more straightforward and shocking way.

Black and White and Red All Over: Frank Miller's *Sin City*

Miller's first major works for Dark Horse were noirish visions of the future, first appearing in 1990: *Give Me Liberty* (the beginning of the Martha Washington series) with Dave Gibbons as illustrator, and *Hard Boiled* with Geof Darrow as illustrator. Although the Martha Washington series showcased Miller's libertarian sense of the United States, *Hard Boiled* is more significant in terms of the increasing crime story focus in Miller's career. In a world where systematic corruption runs rampant, the main character lives with the idea that he is an unimpressive insurance investigator (like a variation on Walter Neff in *Double Indemnity*); in fact, he is a violent cyborg that kills anyone who threatens the corporation that created him. After discovering that the robots enslaved by the corporation consider him their savior, he destroys the robots that sought him out and asks the corporation to restore his largely unaware identity as an insurance investigator. With this take on the influence of the power of a corporate system on individual identity, Miller portrays the ultimate end of a corporate one-world philosophy: refusing the call to heroism made by the needy in favor of not only living a life of quiet desperation but also choosing a life of quiet desperation. However, the series that followed (initially debuting in *Dark Horse Presents*) would be the work that more finely tuned Miller's sense of the crime story and heroism and was the most discrete starting point for the return of the "dark night" of crime to comic books: *Sin City*. As Miller describes, "For me, the biggest jump came when I sat down at my board to start *Sin City*... exhausted and existentially confused."[43] With little in the way of genre blending described thus far, *Sin City* ultimately worked like the anthologies of classic crime comics; however, all the stories revolved around Basin City, a place reminiscent of the cities of crime fiction but more depraved than almost any other city portrayed in comics.

At this point, it is important to mention that other straightforward crime stories were not completely absent from the comics scene in the 1970s and 1980s, but they were much more limited in distribution and influence (and quite different from *Sin City*). Originally published in a fanzine in the 1970s, Don McGregor and Gene Colan's *Detectives, Inc.* was reworked and published by Eclipse as two graphic novels in 1980 and 1985. Following white and black partners in a private investigation agency, the graphic novels portray their investigations into the life of a wife-beating millionaire and the death of a woman killed by a man in love with her lesbian lover. More widely read was Max Allan Collins and Terry Beatty's *Ms. Tree*, a series beginning in 1981 and initially also published by Eclipse. Following *Ms. Tree*, the hard-boiled detective of the title, the series not only portrays her in pursuit of her husband's killer and her violent entanglements with the mob but also her unexpected pregnancy and her rough times raising her adopted son. Even though Max Allan Collins had name recognition going into the series as the writer who took over for Chester Gould on the *Dick Tracy* comic strip, the series maintained a small but loyal following over the course of a decade as it shifted from one publisher to another. As identified by the film critic Foster Hirsch in *Detours and Lost Highways*, classic crime dealt little with female, black, or homosexual characters (in any way that was not negative) but neo-noir does. In many of these regards, these series worked in connection with the crime novels and films of the contemporary neo-noir movement, aware of the mechanics of noir and intentionally challenging its conventions. *Sin City*, however, would occupy a strange liminal space that evokes classic crime and pushes it forward but serves as much as an homage as a self-conscious exposée of the genre. At this point in his career, Miller stated his sense of the crime story was based more on Chandler, than Spillane (as it had been in the past) and mentions no contemporary works of crime fiction. And in defense of the stereotypical traits of the crime story genre, Miller argued that he saw the pursuit and vengeance motif as a vehicle that could be used to deal effectively with existential themes.[44]

Called *Sin City* and eventually collected as *Sin City: The Hard Goodbye*, the first story of Basin City appeared in the anthology *Dark Horse Presents* in 1991. The protagonist of the series is Marv, a hulking ex-convict who is framed for the murder of Goldie, a prostitute he finds dead in his hotel bed after she spends the night with him free of charge. Moved to avenge her death by the charity of her sexual favor to him, Marv shows himself to be a nearly physically indestructible noir hero as he follows a lead to discover the man responsible for Goldie's murder. From the beginning of the series, the noir connections are created through the story's visual presentation and narrative content. Rendered entirely in the black and white of film noir, Miller alternates between hyperactive attention to detail (such as the endless craggy lines on Marv's face) and simple outlines of seemingly backlit black figures (such as Goldie's naked body on the night she is killed). After Marv tears his way through the police sent to arrest him on the morning of Goldie's murder, Marv's bloody investigation reveals Basin City to not only be filled with sinister lowlifes to beat up for information. His investigation also leads to corruption at the highest levels, involving the Rourke family who control both political and religious sway. With that acknowledgement made, Miller extends the visual conventions of noir with a type of chiaroscuro contrast that further essentializes and emphasizes the dramatic play of light and dark within one figure. For Miller, this is an intentional evocation of illustrators responsible for the best of classic crime comics: "I began thinking simply in terms of areas of black shape. At the same time, I was studying the people who handle black-and-white best in the field. Like Eisner and Wallace Wood and Johnny Craig."[45] Comics creator R.C. Harvey describes his style in this way: "Miller discard[s] the mechanical device of a light source and work[s] purely in black-and-white... Contrast alone shapes the images... And in such circumstances... we see the gambit taken to is logical extreme: here, black becomes, in effect, a 'color,' arrayed against solid white and augmented by fragile linework."[46] His stark contrasts of black and white on the nearly caricatured face of Marv sets realism and abstraction alongside one another and suggests not only a symbol of the split nature of the character but also a darkening of the cartooning style traditionally associated with comic books.

As important in Miller's extension of noir is Marv's psychological instability, fundamentally related to the horrific lengths he goes to see Goldie avenged (violence clearly depicted and far beyond anything previously seen in classic crime comics). Popping pills to keep "the animal in me," as Marv says, he sees Goldie alive after she is killed and wonders, "What if I imagined all this? From Goldie's slow smile to the cop fingering Rourke? What if I finally turned into what they always said I was going to turn into—a maniac, a psycho-killer?"[47] With Marv as narrator and no omniscient, authoritative narrator to clarify the situation, the reader participates in this question about the reality of his experience in a way even more desperate and anxious than Bruce Wayne's struggle portrayed in *The Dark Knight Returns.*

Fig. 3.3
Marv's face is highly stylized as Miller utilizes the play of light and dark without the consideration of a real world light source.
Sin City: The Hard Goodbye, Dark Horse, 1992

Eventually it is revealed that the Goldie that Marv sees is in fact Goldie's twin sister, another prostitute of "Old Town." This revelation removes from Marv his own doubt and allows him to pursue his revenge in extreme and unfettered ways for the illusion of an ideal woman based on his fleeting experience with Goldie. Goldie had learned about a cannibalistic serial killer protected by Cardinal Rourke, who believed the killer found truth, consuming souls in order to become "clean and perfect." (Ironically, the serial killer lives on "the farm," the only hint of an agrarian world outside Basin City but with the killer in residence, the corruption of the city seems inescapable.) Despite Marv's thuggish extremism, he becomes a clear moral center within the story by virtue of contrast. Unlike the hardboiled detective, Marv is relatively free from moral quandaries that might give him pause, and Miller's story extols the virtues of being a criminal in a corrupt world. The ethic of Marv's violent behavior is recommended by Dwight in the next *Sin City* story, *A Dame to Kill For*: "It's... like there's nothing wrong with Marv, nothing at all—except that he had the rotten luck of being born at the wrong time in history. He'd have been okay if he'd been born a couple thousand years ago. He'd be right at home on some ancient battlefield, swinging an ax into somebody's face... They'd have tossed him girls... back then."[48]

The honor and necessity of Marv's extremely violent tendencies (and that of other *Sin City* protagonists) is described by Miller who states, "I believe the violence is necessary, depending on the story. I've always loved horror, and I'm kind of a 'genre mixer,' and one of the things I greatly enjoy doing in a story is replacing catharsis with horror. The way it is in movies and most adventure comics, catharsis is essentially a very satisfying, happy conclusion: the Death Star blows up, whatever. Making that moment terrifying is something I like to play with, so it no longer leaves you feeling all is right with the world."[49] That sense of unease pervades the conclusion of *The Hard Goodbye*; after killing the serial killer and torturing and killing the

Cardinal, Marv is convicted and put on death row, visited only by Wendy, whom he misrecognizes as Goldie. When he is executed in a grisly and disturbing depiction of state sanctioned electrocution, it harkens to the conventional end of most crime stories in *Crime Does Not Pay* with an attitude that distinctly recalls the crime/horror of *Shock SuspenStories*.

Fig. 3.4
Marv's end is far from the contrite end met by most criminals in *Crime Does Not Pay* and actually depicts his capital punishment in a dramatic way. *Sin City: The Hard Goodbye*, Dark Horse, 1992

Black and White and Read All Over: Frank Miller's *Sin City*, Continued

Usually focusing on unstable outsiders drawn into overwhelming situations, subsequent *Sin City* stories play out as catalogues of suffering and tests of masculine endurance. Other installments of *Sin City* feature "quests" by similarly flawed protagonists (Dwight, the scorned boyfriend in *A Dame to Kill For*, Hartigan, the rogue cop in *That Yellow Bastard*, and Wallace, the loner vet in *Hell and Back*). Max Allan Collins described the appeal of these types of characters in crime fiction in this way: "The secret to reader sympathy is no big deal: these men have to be the best men in their world; they live by a code of ethics, within their unethical framework."[50] The triumphant characters of *Sin City* are men who understand the corruption of the city, place no limitations on the violent means used to reach an end, and suppress the sexual desire that might corrupt them. However, as Richard B. Schwartz states in *Nice and Noir*, a sense of unease still accompanies these "sympathetic" characters in noir fiction: "At the same time that we thirst for (sometimes extreme) alternatives,... our responses to the vigilante's brand of violence are heavily nuanced and at times explicitly ambivalent."[51] *The Hard Goodbye* creates a familiar, although extremist, noir environment and subsequent series bring noir types more clearly into play (something that eventually causes readers to question the purpose of Miller's series as homage, criticism, parody, or something else).

In 1993, *A Dame to Kill For* presents Ava as a quintessential femme fatale, drawing Dwight back into their passionate sexual relationship and convincing him to kill her supposedly abusive but rich husband. With the plot abbreviated in this way, her plan for Dwight to take the fall for the murder is obvious, but Miller creates characters rich enough that they simultaneously create a familiar experience and cause the reader to forget conventional expectations of Dwight's fall. Part of the reason for being interested in the routine noir narrative is that Miller doesn't hide it as routine but rather makes it a part of Dwight's inexorable fate. Dwight narrates his return to bed with Ava: "Before long my hatred's spent but she won't let go. She kisses and coaxes me and the fire grows again... We melt together. The shudder runs through both of us. I scream her name... I say all the things I swore I'd never say again. She owns me.

THEY FIX ME A PRETTY DECENT STEAK FOR MY LAST MEAL. THEY EVEN THROW IN A BREW, THE FIRST I'VE HAD SINCE BACK AT NANCY'S.
THEN THEY SHAVE MY HEAD AND FIX ME WITH A RUBBER DIAPER AND GET TO IT.
AND IT'S ABOUT DAMN TIME, IF YOU ASK ME.
YEA, THOUG I WALK THR THE VALLEY OF THE SHAD OF DEATH...
COULD YOU GET A *MOVE ON?* I HAVEN'T GOT ALL *NIGHT!*
YOU HEARD THE MAN. HIT IT.
YES, SIR.

Body and soul."[52] And by representing Dwight's leering gaze on Ava (her naked body seemingly frozen in provocative detail in a long series of panels as she dives into her pool), the reader participates in Ava as Dwight's fantasy. In addition, Miller renders Ava with the look of film noir femme fatales like Ava Gardner or perhaps Rita Hayworth but places her within an illustrative style that, in the arc of *Sin City* tales, becomes less realistic and more stylized. Emphasizing the lines of cigarette smoke surrounding her at the bar or the lines of light falling on them both from blinds as Dwight embraces her, Miller selectively emphasizes typical noir details; excluding the details of the real world that a film camera can't avoid, the series creates a purer experience of noir, a hyper-real noir that makes the old look new.

Fig. 3.5
Gail is Miller's epitome of Sin City's strong and resourceful woman: a prostitute in fetish wear. *Sin City: The Big Fat Kill*, Dark Horse, 1994

While Dwight accepts her scheme and kills her husband, the story doesn't end with Ava shooting Dwight in the face and becoming a rich woman. Instead, Dwight survives, gets a new face from the girls of Old Town who owe him a favor, and assaults Ava's armed compound with the brutal help of Marv (*A Dame to Kill For* taking place before the events of *The Hard Goodbye*). Rather than just expose the fatal flaw of the protagonist in his desire for this sexual, powerful woman, Dwight punishes her for what she did to him and a string of other men. With his new face, Dwight protects the girls of Old Town in *The Big Fat Kill*, who are endangered because they killed a psychopath who, unknown to them, was also a police officer. Extending the mythology of corruption in Basin City, *The Big Fat Kill* reveals that police have a long-standing agreement to stay away from the prostitutes of Old Town. The prostitutes stay in Old Town, take care of their own enforcement, and remain free of men who might want to control them. When this murder threatens this agreement, Dwight agrees to help Gail, the leader of the Old Town prostitutes and his "Valkyrie." On his way to hide the bodies of the police officer and his friends in the tar pits, he finds the dead man talking to him on the car ride there. After overcoming several other obstacles beside his mental instability and including the mob's attempt to move into Old Town, the story ends with Dwight and Gail (with other Old Town girls) enacting and thrilling to the machine gun massacre of the mobsters. Again, Miller sets forth a domineering and unstable hero and supposedly strong but really secondary and sexualized women; and again, he shows violence as a morally acceptable means to face the deepest levels of corruption in an inescapably corrupt world.

WE'VE BEEN ON TOP OF THESE PECKERWOODS SINCE THEY FIRST SHOWED UP WITH THAT COP BEHIND THEM. EVERYTHING'S UNDER CONTROL. SIT BACK AND ENJOY THE SHOW.
THERE'S NO USE ARGUING WITH HER.
THE LADIES ARE THE LAW HERE, BEAUTIFUL AND MERCILESS.
AND THEY'VE GOT THEIR OWN *ENFORCERS*.
THE PLYMOUTH RUMBLES DOWN AN ALLEY THAT FACES NO WINDOWS. JACKIE-BOY'S VOICE RISES TO AN ANGRY, ANNOYING WARBLE.
THE POOR SLOB. I ALMOST FEEL SORRY FOR HIM. HIM AND HIS WHOLE ROTTEN PACK OF LOSERS.
THIS IS GOING TO BE UGLY.

With artistic choices that call attention to the genre, Miller further stylizes crime comics with his graphic depictions of violence and full nudity of women with nearly impossible physical beauty. Miller's hyper-masculine aesthetic eventually came under fire from other industry luminaries such as Alan Moore and mainstream media critics such as Ray Suarez.[53] Of course, Miller's style as a graphic artist developed from one that favored realism and naturalism to one that favored stylization and caricature, and Miller states, "I don't pretend to be doing realistic stories. These are cartoons in every sense of the word."[54] Clearly violating some tenets of visual and narrative realism in Sin City, Miller calls his style "hyperactive" and agrees with Will Eisner's assessment of it as operatic,[55] potentially placing his excesses in the category of camp. To entertain the possibility that Miller takes the genre not so seriously, it becomes important to regard *That Yellow Bastard* (1996) as a turning point in the series.

In some ways echoing Miller's sense of his stories as unrealistic, Raymond Chandler claimed that the hardboiled detective is "an exaggeration–a fantasy, but at least… an exaggeration of the possible."[56] Although the story is that of an ethical and therefore rogue Basin City policeman, Miller essentially reworks the hardboiled detective as presented by Chandler as the lone and frustrated knight of *The Big Sleep*. Beginning at a point in Basin City history before any of the other *Sin City* stories, *That Yellow Bastard* features John Hartigan, a retiring policeman who desperately wants to close a kidnapping case. With a monologue indicating he knows his actions will ruin his comfortable retirement, Hartigan tracks down eleven-year-old Nancy Callahan before she is raped by her kidnapper, the politically protected son of Senator Rourke. His bad heart almost prevents him from cutting down Junior's thugs, but Hartigan does so and shoots Junior to pieces. Hartigan is then shot by his corrupt partner but saves Nancy, whom he feels cuddle close to his hulking frame as his life drains away.

The crime story clichés run rampant herein and it contains much less moral ambiguity than might be found in one of Chandler's Phillip Marlowe stories. However, Miller's continued stylistic innovations keep the narrative interesting, such as placing us within the subjective experience of Hartigan as his heart almost fails him. A single panel presenting him clutching his chest is featured in isolation, surrounded by the black space of an entire page; followed on the next page by another smaller panel presenting him with a more agonized facial expression; and followed by an entirely black page presenting only a text box with his monologue, "Not now." The subsequent page presents several panels depicting Junior making preparations for his uninterrupted time with Nancy, but that disturbing sequence is followed by another black page with the word

"No," and yet another page showing Hartigan pulling himself back to consciousness. More important than the stylistic innovations is the fact that Hartigan becomes, like other *Sin City* heroes, a man risen from the dead again, after his partner shoots him; he is a dirty savior in an even dirtier world.

Hartigan is brought back to life by Senator Rourke's surgeons so that he might be jailed in disgrace, and during his time in prison he corresponds with Nancy, who writes to him under an alias. Unexpectedly, he is visited by Junior, also saved by Rourke's surgeons, but saving his life required even more extreme measures, turning him into a yellow-skinned freak. Tricking Hartigan into pleading guilty so that he might have an early release and find Nancy, Hartigan unwittingly leads Junior to Nancy, now a stripper of gravity-defying beauty. Initially, Nancy declares her love for Hartigan and tries to seduce him despite his protests. In short order, Junior again kidnaps Nancy, and Hartigan escapes certain death to again rescue her and beat Junior to death; where before he shot Junior in the crotch, this time he tears off Junior's penis with his hands. Knowing that Senator Rourke will again want revenge against him and will go through Nancy to have that revenge, Hartigan shoots himself in order to close the loop and protect her. As scholar Christopher Pizzino argues, almost everything in *That Yellow Bastard* seems to take noir conventions to their extremes:

> The cruelty of the torture Hartigan endures, the brutality of the violence he must commit, and the shock of Nancy's attempt to seduce him have a recognizable noir lineage, but the shapes of the narrative elements are bolder and their proportions are magnified... To the degree that Miller draws conscious attention to [the stereotypes] of genre, *That Yellow Bastard* can be seen as an instance of postmodern aesthetics.[57]

Certainly, Miller had engaged in broad parodic gestures in the past *Sin City* stories (such as the Wolverine lookalike whom Marv regularly beats up) but the idea that he may be recommending and targeting noir at the same time had also always been there due to his excessiveness.

This may be more notable in the case of *That Yellow Bastard* with the reconstructed Junior colored yellow to color in an otherwise black-and-white design scheme; in addition, Junior is highly abstracted and seems to be represented in a style unlike the rest of series: "Miller's rendering of Junior the Yellow Bastard suggests a perverse combination of Golden Age American cartooning and 1960s underground comix."[58]

THIS GUY SMELLS AWFUL.

The contrast between these styles of representation may draw attention to each as a style rather than reality, but the grotesque of Junior may also serve a very specific narrative purpose: to deal with the fear that the hero and villain might be similar. "The uncertainty as to where the threat lies (in Nancy's sexuality or in Hartigan himself) points to a problem at the core of Hartigan's paternalistic protection of Nancy, which has either inspired her desire or is an attempt to cover up Hartigan's own. Junior's function is ostensibly to suppress this dilemma, but in transforming his villain into a monstrous Other, Miller disrupts the function by a kind of overfulfillment."[59]

Fig. 3.6
Junior, the yellow bastard, is drawn in a style in stark contrast to Hartigan and the rest of *Sin City*. *Sin City: That Yellow Bastard*, Dark Horse, 1996

This leads Pizzino to ultimately conclude that Miller doesn't call attention to the cliché typology within crime fiction but creates an alternate mode of presentation that adds a false sense of depth to it (or as Rodman argues, the *Sin City* series "transcends fabrication to become [its] own redefined truth"[60]). Miller has certainly defended his genre of choice vehemently[61] and does understand it as an important means to comment upon the dangers of centralized power in modern civilization. In *Family Values*, a 1997 *Sin City* graphic novel, Miller addressed what he considered the hollow rhetoric of those who seek to maintain such power: "I got sick of hearing about family and values and children all the time, so I thought, 'Yeah, let's take a look at what families are.' So first you meet the mafia boss, and then a corrupt politician, and this alcoholic single mother character who's kind of pathetic but obviously concerned about her kid. Ultimately, the family that [the story] most counts for is a pair of lesbians, one of whom is accidentally killed during an assassination."[62]

In addition to this politically conscious gesture toward something like neo-noir, the last work in the *Sin City* series, *Hell and Back*, entertains a postmodern question of whether this serious vehicle for social criticism might be regarded as a thing to be appreciated in itself and also an absurdist fiction by a biased author. In the midst of a desperate attempt to save a woman from a slavery ring (and their programmer Dr. Wertham), Wallace is injected with a drug that gives him full-color hallucinations of Frank Miller's disparate points of inspiration: Hagar the Horrible and Lone Wolf and Cub, Dirty Harry and Captain America, Moses and Hellboy, as well as various Frank Miller creations (Elektra, Martha Washington, etc.). Regardless, the most important part in *Hell and Back* might be another obvious crossing between the fictitious and the real; the evil programmer, Dr. Wertham, is killed by what the 1954 congressional testimony of Fredric Wertham suggested he feared most: a needle to the eye.

Paving the Way to the Rough Road:
Controversy and the Outlaw Aesthetic

Like Motter and Chaykin, Miller begins his journey toward noir in the 1980s with work that blends the crime story with another genre. Also, like Motter and Chaykin, Miller lives in cynical times and reacts with skepticism to the idea of a redemptive hero. However, Miller's influential noir work extends beyond his superhero crime work with the more orthodox crime fiction of *Sin City*, almost singlehandedly reviving the genre in the 1990s. Unlike Chaykin, who identifies himself as a bleeding heart liberal,[63] Miller is often read through his *Sin City* work as an extremely conservative voice. Looking at the trajectory from *Daredevil* to his later work, Miller referred to his *Daredevil* "Roulette" story as his "last throes of liberal guilt"[64] and Gary Groth would thereafter refer to Miller as a "mugged liberal."[65] As Woody Haut has argued in *Neon Noir*, the social critique of the noir narrative is likely to attract proponents from radically different ends of the political spectrum, ranging from Mickey Spillane (a conservative well known for his hatred of communists) to Raymond Chandler (a liberal targeted by Joseph McCarthy). However, Miller is not so easy to categorize with his reading interests moving from Spillane to Chandler during a period in his career when most readers feel his work became more conservative.

Undoubtedly, his work has always focused on masculine concerns, and he has been unapologetic in regard to his portrayal of women (much like Chaykin). With comments about the impossibility of pleasing feminist critics, he positions himself with other contemporary writers who consider modern civilization to be an attack on masculinity.[66] From the start in *Daredevil*, he creates the scantily clad ninja ex-girlfriend Elektra almost solely as a temptation and an antagonist for Daredevil. Later, by having a young girl serve as the new Robin in *The Dark Knight Returns*, he creates a flat devotee of Batman as a safer object of paternal love. And even later, with multiple appearances of the girls of Old Town, he creates women who are only as strong and self-sufficient as they are sexualized and objectified by their provocative rendering in *Sin City*.[67]

However, critic Nathan G. Tipton has argued that the new Robin may distract from Wertham's notion of homosexuality in Batman and yet still acknowledge it[68] (a doubleness I would suggest is a typical undercurrent of the male bonding in crime fiction). And Pizzino has suggested that during the extended presentation of Nancy's stripper routine, she gazes at the reader and exposes the gratuity as the male reader's fantasy.[69] Undeniably, these tensions are not easy and perhaps impossible to resolve in Miller's work and in crime fiction in general. Still, this desire to present women as either the virgin or the whore (and yet undermine that simplistic dichotomy) is a fundamental part of noir: "This gender dynamic—emphatically returning women to their appropriate place while simultaneously calling into question the categories on which such nostalgic politics is based—is characteristic of hardboiled fiction."[70] According to scholar Erin Smith, hardboiled fiction reveals gender to be performative and therefore, men must overcompensate in the performance of masculinity in order to establish a sense of control in a world that offers them very little.[71] This characterization may explain the design of *Sin City* protagonists, and it may also explain Miller's rhetoric that has become increasingly inflammatory, seemingly conservative, and often undermines his credibility as an intellectual visionary.[72] Miller's conservatism does not fit conveniently into a category defined by the American two-party system as indicated by the previously mentioned rationale for *Family Values* and elsewhere by his fierce criticism of Republican politicians and pundits.[73] Although he may be better characterized as a libertarian, his exact political orientation is not as relevant as his contrarian response to culture. *Sin City* is Miller's nowhere and everywhere, past, present, and future. In the post-industrial era of the 1990s, it became obvious the continued economic growth that enabled the material American dream was disappearing as was the American middle class: the class with whom noir writers have long identified. In an era of what might seem like the pointless debates of media-driven, two-party politics, Miller used his crime comics to cast a critical eye on the rich and powerful who sought to consolidate their power at the expense of so many others.

And for Miller, crime comics are the perfect vehicle for such criticism because they have traditionally been outside the boundaries of cultural approval: "One of the reasons why I think of comics as outlaw is that we've been censor-bait from the get-go. If you look at the proudest years of our history, they tended to be when our material was considered the most offensive—look at EC and the undergrounds—and the low periods, at least creatively, were when we were what everybody thought we were."[74] As Larry Rodman would argue, "Dr. Fredric Wertham, the Comics Code and Miller's various employers' acquiescence to this repression are his origin-trauma, his goad and the source of his obsession."[75] Of course, the 1980s saw comic books move off the newsstand and into the comic book stores; they became collectors' items, were discussed in classrooms as art, and in general became much more respectable. But as this took place, Miller's passionate advocacy and extension of the crime comics' controversial content would become more pressing.[76] "[Now that comics have] definitely been proven as an art form… [w]e don't need to keep rationalizing our existence. Now, I think we're on the offensive culturally."[77]

In many ways, it is essential that his crime comics remain outside the boundaries of cultural approval so that his judgmental voice (as a critically approved, award-winning comic superstar) might remain genuine.[78] In Miller's understanding, the excessive violence of crime comics is a means to explore moral problems; his reinterpretation of criminal psychology has the potential to break through the static and thereby effectively present his alternative (albeit hyper-real) vision for justice. Although cited alternately as an indulgent fetish for base desire and as a mirror revealing the underbelly of American culture, *Sin City* undeniably paved the way for a new wave of crime comics: an extremist and counter-cultural return to crime comics roots. And the crime comics that followed in the next decade would follow in his footsteps, but while they questioned culture at large, they would much more obviously question the genre and the medium itself.

Chapter 3 Notes

1 Elvis Mitchell, "Frank Miller Interview on SoCal's KCRW," *Comic Book Resources*, last modified March 30, 2005, http://www.comicbookresources.com/?page=article&id=4820.

2 Bradford W. Wright, *Comic Book Nation: The Transformation of Youth Culture in America* (Baltimore: Johns Hopkins University Press, 200 1), 84–185.

3 Randy Duncan and Matthew Smith, *The Power of Comics: History, Form, and Culture* (New York: Continuum, 2009), 43.

4 Ibid., 46.

5 Wright, *Comic Book Nation*, 212.

6 This story points out one of the most obvious problems with the code (condemning certain types of behavior without fully identifying them); it became a central reason for the loosening of the code in 1970s.

7 Stanley Wiater and Stephen R. Bisette, *Comic Book Rebels of the New Comics: Conversations with the Creators* (New York: Dutton, 1993), 218–219.

8 George, *Frank Miller: The Interviews: 1981–2003*, 15.

9 Ibid., 18.

10 Ibid., 23.

11 Ibid., 20.

12 One of Wally Wood's final jobs would be inking Frank Miller's cover of *Daredevil* No. 164.

13 George, *Frank Miller: The Interviews: 1981–2003*, 21.

14 Frank Miller, *Daredevil: Visionaries 2* (New York: Marvel Comics, 2001), 330.

15 Greg S. McCue and Clive Bloom, *Dark Knights: The New Comics in Context* (London: Pluto Press, 1993), 69.

16 Tim Blackmore, "Blind Daring: Vision and Revision in *Oedipus Tyrranus* and in Frank Miller's *Daredevil: Born Again,*" *Journal of Popular Culture 27* (Winter 1993): 138.

17 Wright, *Comic Book Nation*, 267.

18 Ibid., 273.

19 McCue and Bloom, *Dark Knights*, 69.

20 Frank Miller, Batman: *The Dark Knight Returns* (New York: DC Comics, 1996), 13.

21 Ibid., 13.

22 George, *Frank Miller: The Interviews: 1981–2003*, 33.

23 Jesse W. Nash, "Gotham's Dark Knight: The Postmodern Transformation of Arthurian Mythos," *Popular Arthurian Traditions*, ed. Sally K. Slocum (Bowling Green KY: Bowling Green State Popular Press, 1992), 41.

24 Miller, Batman: *The Dark Knight Returns*, 55.

25 George, *Frank Miller: The Interviews: 1981–2003*, 35.

26 Miller, *Batman: The Dark Knight Returns*, 139.

27 Tim Blackmore, "The Dark Knight of Democracy: Tocqueville and Miller Cast Some Light on the Subject," *Journal of American Culture* 14 (Spring 1991): 39.

28 Ibid., 53.

29 Ibid., 55.

30 McCue, and Bloom, *Dark Knights*, 70.

31 Peter S. Prescott, "The Comic Book (Gulp!) Grows Up," *Newsweek*, January 18, 1988, 71.

32 George, *Frank Miller: The Interviews: 1981–2003*, 34.

33 Ibid., 51.

34 Ibid., 53.

35 Duncan and Smith, *The Power of Comics*, 120–121.

36 George, *Frank Miller: The Interviews: 1981–2003*, 52.

37 Ibid., 42.

38 Charles Brownstein, *Eisner/Miller* (Milwaukie, OR: Dark Horse, 2005), 116–117.

39 George, *Frank Miller: The Interviews: 1981–2003*, 53.

40 Ibid., 51.

41 Ibid., 60.

42 Brownstein, *Eisner/Miller*, 214.

43 George, *Frank Miller: The Interviews: 1981–2003*, 91.

44 Brownstein, *Eisner/Miller*, 97.

45 George, *Frank Miller: The Interviews: 1981–2003*, 81.

46 R. C. Harvey, "When Less is More, An Entire City: An Introduction," *The Art of Sin City*, by Frank Miller (Milwaukie, OR: Dark Horse, 2002), 4.

47 Frank Miller, *Sin City: The Hard Goodbye* (Milwaukie, OR: Dark Horse, 1993), 134.

48 Frank Miller, *Sin City: A Dame to Kill For* (Milwaukie, OR: Dark Horse, 1995), 93.

49 Wiater and Bisette, *Comic Book Rebels of the New Comics*, 223.

50 Arune Singh, "Just the Facts Ma'am: Max Collins Talks Road to Perdition," *Comic Book Resources*, last modified June 16, 2002, http://www.comicbookresources.com/?page=article&id=1193.

51 Richard B. Schwartz, *Nice and Noir: Contemporary American Crime Fiction* (Columbia, MO: University of Missouri Press, 2002), 27.

52 Miller, *Sin City: A Dame to Kill For*, 63–65.

53 Moore would write an introduction to *The Dark Knight Returns* but has become increasingly critical of *Sin City* over the years; on "Talk of the Nation," Suarez began his May 1995 interview with Scott McCloud on the topic of adult comics by indicting them with the content of *Sin City*.

54 George, *Frank Miller: The Interviews: 1981–2003*, 72.

55 Brownstein, *Eisner/Miller*, 96.

56 Gardiner, Dorothy and Katherine Sorley Walker, *Raymond Chandler Speaking* (Berkeley: University of California Press, 1997), 60.

57 Christopher Pizzino, "Art That Goes Boom: Genre and Aesthetics in Frank Miller's *Sin City*," *English Language Notes* 46 (November, 2008): 117–118.

58 Ibid., 122. In fact, Junior, as the Yellow Bastard, looks like a disgusting and corrupted full-grown version of everyone's favorite plucky city-dweller, Outcault's the Yellow Kid.

59 Ibid., 123.

60 Larry Rodman, "New Blood: A Frank Miller Career Overview," *Frank Miller: The Interviews: 1981–2003*, ed. Milo George (Seattle: Fantagraphics, 2003), 129.

61 George, *Frank Miller: The Interviews: 1981–2003*, 90.

62 Brownstein, *Eisner/Miller*, 89–90.

63 Gary Groth and Robert Fiore, *The New Comics: Interviews from the Pages of* The Comics Journal (New York: Berkley, 1988), 86.

64 Wiater and Bisette, *Comic Book Rebels of the New Comics*, 222.

65 Groth and Fiore, *The New Comics*, 59.

66 Foster Hirsh, *Detours and Lost Highways: A Map of Neo-Noir* (New York: Limelight, 1999), 8.

67 At the same time his work in *Sin City* began to draw fire for its sexism, the series continued to win Eisner awards.

68 Nathan G. Tipton, "Gender Trouble: Frank Miller's Revision of Robin the *Batman: Dark Knight Series*," *The Journal of Popular Culture* 41 (2008): 330–331.

69 Pizzino, "Art That Goes Boom," 120.

70 Erin A. Smith, *Hard-Boiled: Working-Class Readers and Pulp Magazines*, 41.

71 Ibid., 161.

72 Although it extends beyond the time period strictly covered in this chapter, many see this in Miller's isolationist stance on NPR's "This I Believe" and his "Anarchy" tweet against the Occupy Wall Street movement.

73 George, *Frank Miller: The Interviews: 1981–2003*, 115–117.

74 Ibid., 94.

75 Rodman, "New Blood: A Frank Miller Career Overview," 125.

76 Undoubtedly, Miller was relieved by the bursting of the collector culture bubble in the 1990s.

77 Brownstein, *Eisner/Miller*, 178.

78 "Still considered low-brow and throwaway [in the 1950s], hardboiled writing has remained marginal in its relationship to mainstream literary criticism" (Woody Haut, *Pulp Culture* [London: Serpent's Tail, 1996], 3).

CHAPTER 4

After Dark (Another Generation of Comic Noir): Brian Michael Bendis, Brian Azzarello, and Ed Brubaker

The art of cinematography is really the art of telling a story with images and using the light and color and shadows to express more than is even being said, so that stuff gets under my skin more than anything.
Brian Michael Bendis[1]

I wanted the violence to hurt—to actually have some consequence—I suppose that was just a reaction to comic books in general, super hero comic books. They beat the shit out of each other with no consequences at all.
Brian Azzarello[2]

What if I did a story about these characters from this made-up, analogue version of a kid's comic, who all grew up? But they grew up fucked-up, because they grew up exactly like Dr. Wertham's worst fears of what kids reading comics would be.
Ed Brubaker[3]

Beyond the Direct Market: Art and the Outlaw Aesthetic

As the direct market became more important to both the independent publishers and the big two, new opportunities became a standard expectation among new talent in the early 1990s. With independent successes as wide ranging as *Love and Rockets*, *American Flagg!*, *Maus*, and *Sin City,* creators were often encouraged to experiment with content and form by publishers such as Fantagraphics Books (the publishing house associated with *The Comics Journal*). The issue of creators' rights became so important that it led to an exodus of major talent from the big two to newly established creator-owned imprints like Image Comics. However, most publishers wanted to be financially successful and recognized that there was more money and success in imitating innovations of the past than in breaking new ground. As DC and Marvel supposedly became edgier, they continued to grind out pretty standard superhero stories that just happened to have more sex and violence.

And as Image supposedly gave ownership of creative properties to creators, they ground out pretty standard superhero stories that just happened to have more sex and violence. Within this best of times/worst of times scenario within the direct market, many publishers took advantage of a growing number of buyers in a way that would lead to the bust of the direct market model. Many of the buyers, both readers and non-readers, were attracted to comic books as collectibles, and publishers would put out many variant editions of each issue (forcing buyers to purchase multiple copies of the same issue). When it became apparent to collectors that print runs of one million issues would never lead to significant resale profit, the buying audience for comic books radically decreased in 1992 and 1993 (the era of the "Death of Superman").[4]

As publishers subsequently sought new marketing strategies, comic book series were more often collected as book-bound graphic novels for the mainstream bookstore. The short-lived growth of the comic book store paved the way for the realization of Will Eisner's dream of the graphic novel, and the medium moved toward cultural respectability with authors such as Art Spiegelman and Chris Ware. Major newspapers and mainstream periodicals like *Entertainment Weekly* began regularly reviewing comic book series and graphic novels. Authors like Dean Motter, Howard Chaykin, and especially Frank Miller benefited from this transition made in the late 1990s, but ultimately it became just another phase in the development of crime comics. As the audience for comic books shrunk further, old and new publishers became more careful with their commitments to new creators, and whatever spirit of risk had been part of the direct market was lost.

With that stated, *Sin City* had demonstrated a market for crime comics and Miller's innovative visual design lent artistic respectability to something that otherwise might be dismissed as just genre material. Eventually, this popularity and critical acclaim led DC, the darling of the Comics Code era, to put out an imprint in their adult-oriented Vertigo line exclusively devoted to crime. From 2001, most comic book publishers were abandoning the review of the Comics Magazine Association of America entirely as the comic book readership skewed much older.[5] The public at large and Congress had turned its fears of new media (and their own children) to the newer scapegoats of popular music in 1980s and video games in the 1990s. This doesn't mean that crime fiction had lost either its widespread popularity or its taboo-breaking controversy (as noted with *Sin City*, crime fiction continued to violate polite standards of acceptability). And that taboo breaking seemed to become of greater interest in an era built on "the cynicism of forty years of the Cold War, nuclear unrest, fiscal uncertainty, and the sexual revolution."[6] In his "map" of neo-noir,

Foster Hirsch argues that neo-noir of the 1980s and 1990s works with and beyond a pastiche style based on self-awareness to again reveal an unspecific fear of being.[7] In many ways, this trajectory can be seen from within the classic era of crime fiction, with the self-consciousness of the hardboiled detective's whip-smart sarcasm. Moreover, the self-consciousness of the rules that governed the genre has led to pastiches and near-parodies of the past (like *The Big Sleep*[8] and *Touch of Evil*)[9] to now be considered classic examples of the film genre. Conspiracy fear in American culture after events like Watergate, the Iran-Contra affair, and the Waco standoff caused many to question the driving forces in behind it all; in response, neo-noir would boldly expose the conceits of modern culture (including the medium itself) and thereby function as a more complex critique of post-industrial society. This somewhat postmodern approach applies in limited degrees to Dean Motter, Howard Chaykin, and Frank Miller, but in much greater degrees to the next era of comic noir creators: Brian Michael Bendis, Brian Azzarello, and Ed Brubaker.

Organized Crime: Neo-Noir in Novels and Film

Although the term neo-noir is often used to describe the crime films that post-date the classic noir period (like Roman Polanski's *Chinatown*), the term has come to be used also to describe crime novels that post-date pulp fiction and the authors who worked within and beyond the pulp magazines. With that stated, dating neo-noir prose is often very difficult as the careers of Jim Thompson and Patricia Highsmith overlap that of Raymond Chandler and Mickey Spillane, but their focus seems to indicate an evolutionary development in crime fiction (the criminal versus the hardboiled detective). While Thompson and Highsmith both demonstrate an awareness of the genres in which they work, the purpose of exposing the conceits of crime fiction is more fully realized with other authors such as Elmore Leonard and Ed McBain. Like Thompson and Highsmith, Elmore Leonard demonstrated a clear sense of what makes an ordinary person into an extraordinary criminal in works such as *52 Pickup*. However, he eventually moved beyond this type of criminal-next-door plot reminiscent of *Crime Suspenstories*. Demonstrating an awareness of the crime story conventions that borders on parody, *Get Shorty* (1990) follows a low level Miami loanshark in his attempt to sell Hollywood a script based on his own experiences; with his criminal activities continuing in Hollywood, it becomes apparent that he is still living his script and laments the difficulty of writing a good ending.

Ed McBain became famous for his pioneering "87th Precinct" series but became critically renown under the name Evan Hunter with novels such as *The Blackboard Jungle*. Although many writers have worked in different genres, McBain and Hunter worked in the same genre but approached it from different perspectives: respectively, the taut thrills of the police procedural and the psychological realism of the crime novel. The illusion of the pseudonym became more than a practical device for McBain who wanted to work in more than one way when McBain and Hunter joined as partners to write *Candyland* (2000). Juxtaposing their different approaches in a gritty story of a prostitute's murder, this stunt suggested a metafictive approach to the ideas of fiction and realism. Perhaps the most radical interrogation of crime fiction in the neo-noir period would be Paul Auster's *City of Glass* in which a detective fiction writer becomes a private investigator and loses his grip on reality; however, this loss (consistent with the assault on personal identity in hardboiled detective fiction) paves the way for some awareness that the character is part of a fiction crafted by Paul Auster.[10]

Like *Touch of Evil*, many of the neo-noir films follow genre rules to such a degree that the films, on one hand, work dramatically, but on the other, expose themselves as an auteur's exercise in style; these include the Coen brothers' *Blood Simple* (1984) as a study in criminal psychology and *Miller's Crossing* (1990) as a gangster tragedy, as well as John Dahl's *Red Rock West* (1994) with a small time crook in over his head and *The Last Seduction* (1994) with a femme fatale manipulating her men. Brian DePalma's *Body Double* (1984) combines and reworks the plots of *Rear Window* and *Vertigo* (films that had already reworked noir) and added graphic sex and violence. Moreover, it takes a conventional noir plot of the confidence scheme and portrays both the mark and, to some degree, the con man as Hollywood actors. In the end, it becomes more than unclear what plot elements are real and what are drawn from cheap B-grade Hollywood films.

And perhaps the most significant of the new wave of crime films is Quentin Tarantino's *Pulp Fiction* (1994) with a title that's meant to evoke the questionable source material not just in prose but also film (with Tarantino also drawing on other more recent questionable film traditions such as the grind house cinema). With hip, clever, and fast-talking hit men as protagonists, the film presents overlapping stories filled with pop culture references that made the criminal life both exciting and banal. Despite the fact that all of the questionably moral characters were humanized, they all seemed to be intentionally or unintentionally enacting roles prescribed by them for a culture of gangsters and tough guys and evoking the bitter laughter of black humor. And with dialogue that demonstrated the characters' own self-consciousness alongside an innovative non-linear structure, the film clearly mixed so-called low culture with conventions of the art film.

As film critic Paul Monaco argues, neo-noir is "knowingly allusive, richly intertextual, yet increasingly the fictive universe of the late 1940s and 1950s they invoke… is constructed only through and out of the same allusive gestures themselves."[11]

With all this self-awareness and postmodern technique clearly becoming important, some neo-noir work changed noir in simpler and perhaps more profound ways by moving beyond the focus on straight white men. Sara Paretsky with V.I. Warshawski and Sue Grafton with Kinsey Millhone present female hardboiled detectives. Walter Mosley presents a black hardboiled detective with Easy Rawlins. Dan Kavanaugh presents a bisexual hardboiled detective in *Duffy*, and Neil Jordan presents a black, transsexual femme fatale in *The Crying Game*.

However, before V.I. Warshawski and Kinsey Millhone, Max Allan Collins's Ms. Tree made her debut with Eclipse in 1981, a forerunner for two of Brian Michael Bendis's most important series: *Jinx* and *Alias*. Each issue of the regular series featured a pin-up of a famous detective, starting with Mike Hammer and provided by Frank Miller, an aspiring new artist and fan of noir fiction. In a way that demonstrated the novelty of Ms. Tree as a female hardboiled detective, the one pin-up Miller provided of a female detective was that of the squeaky clean, safe-for-adolescents Nancy Drew. The protagonist, Michael Tree (significantly a woman with a traditionally male name), takes over her husband's private investigation agency when he is murdered by the Muerta organized crime family. Part of the series is spent on the cases brought to the agency, and part of the series is spent on the aftermath of her husband's death, which includes her tracking down his killer. Envisioning Ms. Tree as Mike Hammer's secretary Velda taking over the business, Collins states, "She really is a female version of Mike Hammer, but she's smarter than Mike."[12] Tracking down the murderer of a partner is a hardboiled detective cliché, and Ms. Tree's body count is at least as high as the number seen in Hammer novels. However, Ms. Tree is more than Mike Hammer in drag with the story turning toward more distinctly female concerns. Then the writer for the *Dick Tracy* comic strip, Collins stated, "'Ms. Tree' was created in part to do the topics that were too hot for 'Tracy'–abortion, clinic bombings, gay bashing, date rape, etc."[13] In that short list he provides, the topics are not only controversial issues and off-limits for a broader family audience but also are related to "others" such as women and homosexuals not regarded with sympathy in traditional hardboiled fiction. Furthermore, Ms. Tree would directly deal with issues of parenthood with her stepson and eventually of pregnancy as the unexpected consequence of sex with the wrong man.

With both Collins and the illustrator, Terry Beatty, citing Johnny Craig's EC work as inspiration,[14] they maintained the oppressive and paranoid atmosphere of traditional crime fiction; in one of the earliest stories, Ms. Tree discovers that both her new lover and psychologist are involved in a criminal conspiracy against her. Regardless, their stated intention was to move beyond an excessive devotion to tradition: "[W]e immediately rejected certain private-eye-story clichés… all the trappings that seemed to us the makings of pastiche and unintentional parody."[15] Despite this claim about avoiding pastiche and parody, Ms. Tree's violation of masculine clichés may have inadvertently led to some of the self-conscious pastiche seen in the series over the years. And this move toward pastiche and an examination of the genre itself is not unexpected as suggested by Hans Bertens and Theo D'Haen in *Contemporary Crime Fiction*: "[W]ith female PI's… they are aware of one important source of power [their voice] and that they are willing to cross gender lines in order to make it available to themselves… [W]e have women looking at men, or, even better, narrators who are aware of their narrative power and subject it to scrutiny."[16]

In an homage to mystery radio shows and crime comics of the past, *Ms. Tree* featured hokey "minute mysteries" as a back-up feature, but eventually the star of that feature appeared on a semi-regular basis in *Ms. Tree*'s qualitatively more sinister world. Reprints of Johnny Danger later became another back-up feature, and Danger also would become a short-term (and clearly much older) character in a *Ms. Tree* storyline. With a cult following, *Ms. Tree* moved from Eclipse to Aardvark-Vanaheim/Renegade and eventually became a quarterly publication from DC, ending its run in the early 1990s. Although not popular enough to be collected as graphic novels, *Ms. Tree* is fondly remembered as a unique title by many crime comics fans and denizens of the direct market comic book store. Involved in the direct market scene in various ways, Bendis, Azzarello, and Brubaker were part of a new generation coming to comics with less of a need to validate their medium or their genre. And like Collins, they maintained some rules of the crime fiction genre and revised others in what amounts to not only a crime fiction critique of society but also a critique of crime fiction. Whereas classic crime comics claimed to present true stories, their work contains self-conscious meta-fictive elements that immediately call into question the accuracy of the facts and the realness of reality. Whether looking through the eyes of an unexpected criminal, mixing narrative and visual styles in obvious ways, or rewriting the past with a pathologically skewed perspective, these stylized stories make their dangerous world a hyper-real experience for readers.

Seeing in the Pale Light: Brian Michael Bendis's *A.K.A. Goldfish*, *Jinx*, and *Torso*

Bendis's first work in comics was not in illustration or writing but in sales at a comic book store where he was immersed in the direct market culture as a reader of superhero and crime comics. Though Bendis arrived on the scene at a time very different from when Frank Miller broke into the business, their careers have notable similarities but also notable dissimilarities. Bendis's primary inspirations were crime comics, crime novels, and film noir; beginning as an illustrator with a love for crime comics, he eventually devoted more attention to his work as a writer. However, his inspirations were much more contemporary, including Howard Chaykin in crime fiction, Richard Price in fiction, and David Mamet in film, favoring all of them for their brilliant use of dialogue.[17] Also, the independent scene created a space for a budding young writer/illustrator to produce crime comics (with Bendis only in later years turning to the big two and superheroes). And while Motter, Chaykin, and Miller were aware of film and all were involved in filmmaking to various degrees, Bendis began with film as a major point of departure in his graphic awareness. In a comment that combines his love and irreverence toward comics, Bendis states, "[Comics is] a bastard medium by its nature. It's constantly pulling stuff into it... What I'm more inspired by is the art of cinematography."[18] In his earliest work, the influence of unique camera angles and lighting were apparent in his tales of conmen and crooks, illustrated figures overwhelmed by the darkness of their surroundings and their lives. With *A.K.A. Goldfish* (1994) and *Jinx* (1996) published by Caliber, Bendis presented stories reminiscent of pulpy crime stories but with the clever, hip, and self-aware dialogue of a Quentin Tarantino film; he also created female characters that evoke the classic femme fatale with a complexity that implies a feminist revisionism of noir fiction.

After refining his use of dialogue in the spy thriller *Fire*, Bendis presented his first mature crime work with *A.K.A. Goldfish*, replete with a smooth-talking conman (David Gold, a.k.a. Goldfish) and a seductive femme fatale. On one hand, the series employs many of the clichés of the crime story, with Gold coming back to town to settle a score and with the over-the-top crime lord running a nightclub that also happens to be a casino and brothel. On the other hand, the series threatens those clichés by stretching them to a breaking point. The femme fatale and the crime lord are one and the same, and she is raising the ten-year-old son she had with Gold (the son revealed as the reason he came back). The references to the culture of the classic crime period make the source material obvious and its implementation ironic: lining the walls of the 1990s nightclub are posters for *42nd Street*, *The Harvey Girls*, and *High Society*, and Gold's ex (the femme fatale/crime lord) is named Lauren Bacall. The black humor of the series is the result of the violation of clichés, made obvious when Bacall discovers a seeming intruder in her office to whom she tells a story of a hat box full of money hidden by her grandmother, a "real old-time mob-girl": "I found an old hat box full of money!... I would daydream at school about it. I would spend it in my head over and over again. And even though my temptation—greater than any I'd ever known... I never took one dollar out of that box. Y'know why? Because I knew if I did—my grams would know. And if I was lucky—she'd break my arm... And it wouldn't matter if I got up the nerve to tell on her or not—nobody listens to little kids."[19] In the panel that concludes her story, the intruder is revealed to be her son (and the story is meant as parental advice). And in the background, a poster for *The G Men* hangs as another period piece, and with the film's faith in violent but benevolent authority figures, it also serves as an ironic counterpoint. With this comic exaggeration of the criminal ill fit for parenthood, Bacall works within and beyond the cliché, occupying some of the space reserved for the femme fatale but also some of the space reserved for the man who would be head of a criminal empire.

With a clever three-card monte structure to *A.K.A. Goldfish*,[20] the reader is kept unaware of Gold's long con and finds the story playfully undermining expectations for the crime story. At the same time, Bendis does not treat Gold just as an ironic vehicle for his critique of noir, but manages to develop a genuine depth to the character. In regard to tongue-in-cheek references (like those made by Gold), Bendis states, "I would agree with [Quentin Tarantino]. I don't do ironic pop culture... It's not terribly clever for literature."[21] When Gold's plans go awry and end tragically, the panels that depict him holding the limp, dead body of his son has genuine pathos (due in part to their visual presentation). In many places, including these panels, Bendis illustrates in a style grounded in cinematic realism, based on human models and accented by the long shadows. When Gold speaks to his dead son, his son is front lit, but Gold is seemingly back lit, becoming nothing but a black outline and negative space. In addition, Bendis slowed and nearly froze time in the shoot out that led to the death of his son and of Bacall. In a series of panels that zoom toward Bacall's suddenly frightened face, Bendis humanizes the seemingly crazed gun moll in the microseconds before her death. Even though Gold avoids the authorities and leaves with a different boy orphaned by the shoot out, the story is still one of the desperation of human existence.

The last portion of the story is tied to the interrogation of a corrupt detective whose gay lover was Bacall's henchman and killed in the final confrontation between Gold and Bacall. After he finishes telling the story to the police (again), he tells the story of a tailor handpicked by JFK to furnish him with all his suits. After the tailor sold his business to move to Washington, JFK was assassinated, and no one in his office remembered the promise that the president made to the tailor. According to the corrupt detective, people hear the story and identify it as an interesting story about JFK, and then he yells: "When the hell is it my God-damn turn?!!! When is the fucking story about me?!! I lost, too, y'know! I lost everything!!! And all I hear about is fucking God-damn Goldfish!" And the interrogator pauses over several panels and then says, "Let' start over…"[22]

Continuing his exploration of women in crime stories, Bendis produced *Jinx*, a prequel to *A.K.A. Goldfish*, featuring Gold as a major character and love interest for the protagonist, a bounty hunter nicknamed Jinx. With a story structured around the big reveal of the meaning of an image on the first few pages of the series, Jinx eventually tells Gold about it: the time she saw money fly through the air. When a bounty takes her gun and shoots her, Jinx chases him down, past the horror of the bodies that he leaves in his path, and beats him. The beating causes his satchel, full of money, to burst, and she says, "I turn into a Pavlov dog. I just go 'woo hoo… look at all the money!!' Disgusting… and I know what you're going to say. Hey! It was just a reflex. A slip… It was just a momentary lapse… But don't you see? It's times like this one… It's times like these when you find out what you're really made of."[23] Employing long shadows to cover Jinx's features as she retreats into her own shame, Bendis also structures panels irregularly, as shards, to represent the fractured nature of Jinx's experience in her own mind.

Although Jinx wants to be better than the violence and greed of the streets, she works with Gold in an unexpected opportunity for big money. Gold must work with a former partner to gather information and find the money in question, but that dim-witted partner is set against Gold and on the verge of killing him. It is as this dim-witted former partner that Bendis inserts himself into the story (modeling the visual design of the character on himself), a clever inside joke that undermines his authority as the story's creator. In fact, Jinx's notebook of fictional stories becomes source material for a fantasy story that at one point takes over the comic book narrative; and in a departure from Bendis's realistic style, in a 1970s style of advertising, illustration, and narrative recap typical in Marvel Comics' Blaxploitation-inspired Power Man, the story is not only recapped but also parodied at an early point in the series. Nevertheless, Bendis again manages to

I SEE--I SEE A LITTLE MONEY FLY THROUGH THE AIR AND I TURN INTO A PAVLOV DOG.
I JUST GO: "WOO HOO... LOOK AT ALL THE MONEY!!"
DISGUSTING...
..AND I KNOW WHAT YOU'RE GOING TO SAY.
HEY! IT WAS A REFLEX. IT WAS A SLIP...
IT WAS JUST A MOMENTARY LAPSE...
BUT DON'T YOU SEE?
IT'S TIMES LIKE THIS ONE..IT'S TIMES LIKE THESE WHEN YOU FIND OUT WHAT YOU'RE REALLY MADE OF.
I MEAN, REALLY MADE OF.
AND YOU KNOW WHAT?
I'M TELLING YOU, I SWEAR, I'M SUPPOSED TO BE BETTER THAN THAT.
THERE'S SUPPOSED TO BE A LOT MORE.
I LOOK AT WHAT I'VE BECOME AND...
AND...
AND...
I HATE MYSELF FOR IT...

maintain the integrity of his characters in the midst of the self-conscious undermining of story and medium conventions. At the end, Jinx and Gold are still well rounded and appealing, and their loss of the big score to the late-appearing Bacall feels like a genuine loss for these sympathetic characters. Regardless, the two still have each other and decide that something other than the score binds them together; of course, this relatively happy ending is ultimately informed by the tragic end of Gold's story as revealed in *A.K.A. Goldfish*.

Fig. 4.1
Jinx's fractured self is reflected in the dark shadows and the off-kilter and fractured panel arrangement
Jinx, Caliber, 1996

While working on *Jinx*, Bendis moved from Caliber to Image, sought by Todd McFarlane to write *Sam and Twitch*, a spin-off series featuring the detectives from McFarlane's *Spawn*. Although set in the superheroic fantasy world of *Spawn*, *Sam and Twitch* took shape as a gritty crime comic.

Regardless, Bendis's next significant contribution to the evolution of comic noir came with *Torso* (1998), co-written with Marc Andeyko and based on the Eliot Ness case of the "torso killer." This series is interesting for several reasons, not the least of which is a return of the true story to crime comics. While Bendis's research into the case was extensive, he was primarily interested in exploring the unknown aspects of the story, ranging from Eliot Ness as a character largely created by the media to the torso killer, whose identity was never revealed. By fleshing out these details for dramatic effect, Bendis and Andeyko participated in a proud crime comics tradition dating back to *Crime Does Not Pay*. However, rather than extol the virtues of authority as early crime comics claimed to do, *Torso* unmakes the myth of Eliot Ness; and as will also be seen with Azzarello and Brubaker, Bendis's work suggests the attempt to represent a "true" story is problematic at best and deserves to be revealed as such. In the showy press conference that introduces him for the first time in the story as Cleveland's new safety director (hopefully a public relations victory for Cleveland), a reporter questions Ness as the man famous for antagonizing but never making a case against Al Capone. While in some ways a police procedural, Ness takes shape as a tragic figure, a good man who wrecks his marriage for a job that has few real rewards for him or positive effects on the community he serves.

With a serial killer at the center of the story, *Torso* moves into territory beyond classic crime and more distinctly neo noir; as Foster Hirsh argues, the serial killer is "the noir equivalent of human monsters in modern horror stories… and threatens generic boundaries."[24] In some ways, this threat to genre is what invigorates neo-noir fiction, with *Torso* including a confrontation between Ness and Gaylord Sundheim, the serial killer too clever to be caught by conventional means. Yet, the story refuses to stray into a psychological explanation of the serial killer in post-industrial society and maintains a more traditional crime comics critique in its explanation of why the killer was never brought to justice. Throughout the story, Ness is stymied by a corrupt political system that keeps the truth from the public; even if Ness had the evidence, he couldn't detain Sundheim, the nephew of a state senator.

Torso is Bendis's most experimental work as an illustrator with unorthodox panel arrangements that make extensive use of negative space and representational figure drawing that ranges from realistic to abstract, depending of the character and situation. For instance, Ness is consistently presented on the realistic side of the spectrum, but other characters might be represented in less accurate detail (like the officer stationed outside the killer's "haunted house") to force greater focus on surrounding details. One of the consistent stylistic choices that synthesizes Bendis's comic book and film sensibility is a telescoping over the course of several panels. Sometimes used to fade into a scene from a pixilated starting point, it is more effectively used to represent the horror of individuals encountering the killer's work. Most important in regard to Bendis's meta-fictive tendencies is his juxtaposition of his own variations in style alongside caricatured representations of the killer (actually used in the Cleveland newspapers in the 1930s) as well as archival photos. Rather than add a sense of realism to the true crime story, it heightens the sense that this graphic novel is a highly constructed intersection between fiction and history.

Figs. 4.2.1
Several images from *Torso* represent the variety of styles employed by Bendis, pushing the reader outside a the typical reality effect of a consistent style
Torso, Image, 1998
© Brian Michael Bendis

Fig. 4.2.2
above
Torso, Image, 1998
© Brian Michael Bendis

Fig. 4.2.3
right
Torso, Image, 1998
© Brian Michael Bendis

Superheroes Beyond the Pale: Brian Michael Bendis's *Alias*

Bendis worked as a writer but not illustrator on *Sam and Twitch*, with Angel Medina providing the highly stylized and moody noir illustration. As inventive as Medina's work often is, Bendis's more significant collaboration at Image was with Michael Avon Oeming on a series beginning in 2000 called *Powers*. The series is a police procedural that follows the cases of Christian Walker and Deena Pilgrim, two detectives in a unit assigned to investigate crimes connected to the superhero population (commonly referred to as powers). With characters that roughly correspond to superhero archetypes created and/or owned by the big two, the detectives explore a decidedly less-than-heroic subculture comprised of people to whom human and natural laws do not apply. In this case, the importance of Oeming's art to the series cannot be overstated; with abstract, simplified figures that resemble classic comic strip illustration, Oeming's illustration works much like Hernandez's illustration in *Mister X*, but in this case alluding to both Gould's *Dick Tracy* and Shuster's *Superman*. However, the intersection is more complex in this case with the profanity, violence, and sex of this other world undermining the tamer worlds of *Dick Tracy* and *Superman*. By turning his crime comics vision to superheroes, Bendis found wider popularity that had thus far eluded him as suggests critic Michael Dean: "[At] the beginning of his career,... his work was ignored by most superhero fans as too unconventional and by alternative-comics aficionados as too genre-bound."[25]

The revising of superheroes continued in more significant ways as Bendis began work with Marvel Comics on several different characters such as Spider-Man (in Marvel's Ultimate Universe) and Daredevil (in Marvel's original universe).[26] Returning *Daredevil* to the crime comics shape created by Frank Miller, Daredevil would again be portrayed as a desperate vigilante; during Bendis's tenure, he would further reveal Murdock's fractured sense of self in society by having him fight against the forces who have publically identified Murdock as Daredevil; as a lawyer, he would openly deny his life as Daredevil, bringing charges against those who might say otherwise.

Eventually, Bendis became a foundational architect for the new shape of Marvel's superhero universe, but his greatest work of crime fiction with Marvel was a noir meta-fiction that even more radically undermined the clichés of superhero mythology: *Alias*. In 2001, *Alias* was the first series published under Marvel's MAX imprint, with the series taking place in the Marvel universe but containing profanity, explicit sex, and graphic violence.

Originally pitched as a series to feature Jessica Drew (Spider-Woman), Bendis created a new character named Jessica Jones whose history would necessarily reshape details of Marvel continuity. (And with the MAX imprint's R-rated content, it was never quite clear how it interacted with the traditional Marvel series.) Formerly a superpowered crime fighter, Jones gave up her superheroic alter ego and became a private investigator. Presented with a Bendis-like gritty perspective, the world of *Alias* is illustrated by Michael Gaydos as dark, dirty, and deeply shadowed, thereby representing Drew as a hardboiled detective. Vestiges of her former life remain, but unlike Miller's *Daredevil,* the crime story doesn't rewrite the superhero story so much as the superhero story stands in almost comic relief against the crime story. In Jones's dingy office, colored almost entirely with earth tones, a picture hanging on the wall features her in a garish pink costume alongside the primary colors of Avengers such as Iron Man and Thor. Roughly a foot shorter than both, the photographer cuts off the heads of the other Avengers in order to center Jones as the superhero Jewel (as if the camera frame can't accommodate A-list heroes in a photo focused on a B-list superhero). This type of character study strongly motivated Bendis: "I guess what I'm more fascinated with, in the case of Jessica, is someone deciding she could never be A-list… It's fun to watch Cap, but what about the person who could never be Captain America?"[27] In this story, superheroes are part of the post-industrial cultural order that makes even other people who are superpowered feel inadequate in the midst of their lives of quiet desperation.

The series begins as Jones informs a client that his wife has cheated, and the man reacts in a way unlikely to be seen by a male gumshoe: her client attacks her. After easily throwing him through her door, she calls the police, who arrive and question her step down in life from superhero to private investigator. Feeling humiliated and generally frustrated, she meets Luke Cage in a bar and works out her frustration in a one-night stand with him. Already, Jones's story has shown that a woman's experience as a private investigator in a crime story environment is quite different from a man's; while the casual sexual encounter might be a regular experience for the hardboiled detective, Jones seems to regard it differently. With her face twisted in something other than pleasure, she narrates, "Lucas will feel guilty about this… But that feeling will pass. Because he'll look back and remember that this was the one night that I let him do anything he wanted. And even though he'll know it's wrong, he'll smile to himself… [But] I don't care what he feels like. I just want to feel something. It doesn't matter what."[28]

Although she uses him for her own ends, she understands him as a fellow human being, and he is more than the useful prop that most men consider women to be in classic crime stories. And later in the series, the encounter has consequences that would never trouble the typical hardboiled detective: an unplanned pregnancy.

As the series continues, the foul-mouthed and flawed Jones turns out to be the knight in blood-caked armor that Miller sees as the hero of noir, often sacrificing her own comfort to protect others (even A-list superheroes like Captain America who make her feel so small). Nevertheless, the Marvel universe as seen and experienced by Jones is a dark place with, among other things, an underground market of "mutant growth hormone," a drug extracted from unwilling mutant donors and sold to addicts seeking the temporary high of superpowers. More importantly, Bendis not only makes the current state of the Marvel universe into this dystopic noir world but revises the past of the Marvel universe to reveal that this darkness is not a recent development. When Jones's superheroic origin is revealed, the artwork makes a radical shift to a style that resembles that of Steve Ditko, who illustrated the earliest Spider-Man stories. Jones went to school with Peter Parker, had a secret crush on the quintessential teenage outsider, and never told him, because the timing of the tragic accident that gave her powers prevented her from telling him. Moreover, that world is not only a place of traumatic origin but also a place without Comics Code enforced innocence; one of the most embarrassing moments in young Jessica's story is when her younger brother interrupts her looking at her poster of the Human Torch and touching herself.

Fig. 4.3
Killgrave talks to Jessica Jones and their existence as comic book characters is revealed by his words and their visual presentation
***Alias*, Marvel, 2003**
© Marvel

In addition to the awkward juxtaposition of these two artistic styles, the story further questions the reader's ability to accept the known experience of superhero comic books as reality. Before Jones retired from her life as the superhero Jewel, her mind was controlled by the supervillain Killgrave, who made her do humiliating and criminal things. When asked by the families of the victims of Killgrave to uncover information about their loved ones, Jones visits Killgrave in prison. She talks to him through a video screen that looks remarkably like a comic book panel, and he begins to narrate her experience (and the experience of the reader) as if contained within a film or comic book: "Interior shot. Jail. Day. Jessica Jones… the ex-costumed superhero, now private eye, comes face-to-face with her greatest foe… tight shot on Jessica. She stares ahead blankly."[29] After Jones tries to steer Killgrave back to her questions, he resorts to a personal attack and the idea that she lives in a comic book world: "You're the biggest whore in the history of the medium!"[30]

Well, you look very purple.
I, uh, I came here to ask you to--
Interior shot. Jail. Day.
Jessica Jones... the ex-costumed super hero, now private eye, comes face-to-face with her greatest foe, her worst nightmare...
...the enigmatic Killgrave, the Purple Man.
...tight shot on Jessica.
She stares ahead blankly...
Trying not to give Killgrave the satisfaction of how much this confrontation is getting to her.
But her eyes are glassy with held back tears. Her quivering lip betrays her.
Even talking through the high-tech prison monitor, even without direct contact of any kind, even with the guards and the security...
...she feels the Purple Man's piercing gaze...
...memories of their intimate time together flushing forward through her. Flooding up inside her.
There are things that they shared that she *never* spoke of...
...even to her lovers.
The truths only *they* know.
Cut to--

While the darkness of Jones's world literally crowds around her in the next few pages in classic noir style, the disruption to the reality of not only the superhero story but also the comic book medium remains. Consequently, when Killgrave escapes and Jones stops him with one big punch, the conventions of the medium have been exposed to such a radical degree that the conventional ending doesn't quite work as a means to stop the threat of evil. Instead, a vague and profound unease persists even as Jones decides to go through with her pregnancy with Luke Cage's support. Whether or not neo-noir works explicitly as a meta-fiction, this feeling of general suspicion of reality and the way things work may be one of neo-noir's most salient features.

Truth Is a Dark Fiction: Brian Azzarello's *100 Bullets*

Like Bendis, Brian Azzarello arrived as part of the new direct market comic book culture, albeit in a more discrete industry position as a line editor for Comico (in its post-bankruptcy revival of the 1990s). Initially having this insider position with a relatively small publisher enabled him to refine his skills as a writer at Comico and then to make a pitch to DC for a series that would help to direct his career. At the time, DC had established the Vertigo imprint as the line more clearly targeting adult readers, almost entirely separated from the DC superhero universe; most titles stood on their own, and even those that didn't, like *Hellblazer* and *Sandman*, leaned away from the superhero genre toward horror and fantasy. When sales of Sandman continued almost unabated after the direct market crash in the early 1990s, DC took the adult line quite seriously as a future tentpole for the company. Azzarello developed a proposal for a crime series featuring *Jonny Double*, based on a Len Wein/Marv Wolfman character from the late 1960s. With the popularity of *Sin City*, he saw it as a prime time to expand the genre base of the Vertigo line. "As far as crime comics, Frank Miller definitely legitimized it… because it was Frank Miller, the book [*Sin City*] showed that this was a viable forum to tell crime stories in."[31]

While *Jonny Double* was only modestly successful, it demonstrated Azzarello's feel for the traditional crime story and his ability to play with the crime story clichés; Double is a private investigator drawn into a money scheme by a beautiful woman, but he is aging and obsessed with 1960s counterculture–the only tie to the classic crime era being the scheme itself: to raid one of Al Capone's safes (perhaps an ironic commentary on the superficial borrowings of contemporary crime writers from the past). Unlike Miller, who most often referred to Raymond Chandler and Mickey Spillane as points of inspiration, Azzarello claimed other crime authors as inspiration for his crime story revisioning: "I'm more of a David Goodis, Jim Thompson, Charles Willeford."[32]

More importantly in reference to *Jonny Double*, this project represented the first collaboration between Azzarello and Eduardo Risso, who would become his long-term collaborator on the most significant crime comic since *Sin City: 100 Bullets*. Running from 1999 to 2009, the popularity of *100 Bullets* clearly established that traditional crime stories had a place within the mainstream comic book publishing industry. "*100 Bullets* came in during the crime and noir craze, and redefined Vertigo from being primarily horror and fantasy to include crime and espionage."[33]

The series initially takes shape like a classic crime comic anthology with isolated stories of people enabled to commit crimes. From the very beginning, the motivational gimmick is Agent Graves and the briefcase he gives to characters: filled with information, a gun, and one hundred untraceable bullets that can be used in any way without fear of prosecution from any law enforcement agency. Bringing the briefcases into the lives of desperate people who have been wronged by others, Graves initially seems like Mr. Crime in *Crime Does Not Pay*, but he is more ambiguous and more literally present (less host and more catalyst). Azzarello admits that he designed Graves to have a Crypt Keeper-like presence, and when asked whether he had EC comics in mind, he responds, "How can you never have that stuff in mind?"[34]

The first story of Isabelle "Dizzy" Cordova is a representative example of many stories in the series, with Dizzy as a gangbanger recently released from prison. Graves meets her to give her the briefcase and the information that her husband and son were killed not in the way she thought but by corrupt police officers. Dizzy initially rejects the absurdity of Graves's untraceable bullets as well as the principle of the revenge that he seems eager to sell in her effort to reform her life. In an imagined conversation with her dead husband, Dizzy tries to work out the cosmic order of things by identifying her husband's and son's deaths as retribution: "Nobody gets away with nothin', do they baby? The man don't understand. When I said your deaths was payback… I meant payback from God."[35] However, Dizzy's return to her old neighborhood leads her back into an environment that sets her against such thinking with old friends still living a life of crime and even her mother telling her to let go of such recrimination: "You gotta move on… If you're weak, you die. Don' be weak baby."[36] Eventually, the dirty police confront Dizzy's brother, Emilio, in her presence and reveal that Emilio set up her husband to be killed because he wanted out of the criminal life. With the police intending to kill both Dizzy and Emilio, she shoots them dead and leaves her brother to take the rap with words of cold comfort: "No matter how bad your life really is… it's still better than being dead."[37] A twisty morality play, the story ends with Mr. Shepherd, an associate of Agent Graves, picking up Dizzy in a large black sedan for a conversation, marking the end of her story and the transition to the next (or so it seems).

However, the seemingly unrelated crime stories in the first year of *100 Bullets* become more clearly related to one another as Agent Graves is developed more as a character, and the 100-bullet briefcases are shown to be part of a larger scheme. A story revealed only in small and implicitly connected pieces, Agent Graves was part of a conspiracy, a soldier working formerly for "The Trust": thirteen crime families that have controlled the United States from its founding. In exchange for complete freedom from interference, the European-based families came to the New World and established themselves as the true controlling power behind the powerful. "The Minutemen" were to be the enforcers (a leader plus seven others) who maintained the balance of power between the thirteen families. When Agent Graves opposed the families who expressed desire to expand their borders and break the centuries-old accord, the Minutemen were disbanded with only one retained as their "warlord," Mr. Shepherd. Since that time, Agent Graves has been operating independently having occasional meetings with Mr. Shepherd and with an agenda directing to whom he gives the one-hundred-bullet briefcases. Although the information in the briefcases is never shown to be fraudulent, it is shown to push people toward revenge that might benefit Agent Graves in his apparent move against the families. Moreover, it is a means by which he sometimes recruits potential members to the Minutemen. While the end of Dizzy's story is initially easy to forget as a bookend that merely takes the reader back to the story gimmick, she reappears as a major character in a series more and more in ways driven by the labyrinthine conspiracy plot. In addition, the information in the briefcases also serves to sometimes reawaken former Minutemen who have had their memories repressed and are now living "ordinary" lives. In fact, the first Minuteman reawakened is working as an ice cream man in an ice cream truck—but nevertheless, he has a desire for revenge in the midst of his seemingly paltry life.

And thus, the rather complicated backstory of *100 Bullets* works to establish that the tendency toward paranoia in typical noir fiction is justifiable based on the reality of a conspiracy. In addition to this criminal conspiracy dating back to the origin of the country and spoiling nostalgia for rich ideals of the past, the conspiracy works to create the fictions that people live and call real. On one hand, that could be routine life prescribed for the mass of humankind, and on the other (or perhaps the same one again), that could be the completely false life given to people like the Minutemen who forget who they once were.

The reawakening of the Minutemen out of the ordinary life of an everyperson has some interesting characteristics that take it beyond the sleeper agent cliché of *The Manchurian Candidate*. Wylie Times is first introduced as a lackadaisical gas station attendant caught up in his friend's small-time scheme to set him up with a better class of criminals. During that scheme, he is protected by Dizzy, and eventually he receives a one-hundred-bullet briefcase identifying Mr. Shepherd as the person responsible for the death of Times's girlfriend, Rose. Again, the information is correct as Rose was a member of one of the crime families, and when she schemes against the families, Mr. Shepherd has Times kill her. While this is certainly information that might reawaken Times to his true identity, it is also information that might lead him to kill Mr. Shepherd. Since the tenor of the relationship between Agent Graves and Mr. Shepherd is ambiguous, Agent Graves might be seeking the latter as much as the former. Regardless, it takes to another level the labyrinthine plots of crime fiction (best represented by Chandler's inability to identify Owen Taylor's murderer in *The Big Sleep*). When Dizzy asks who he is, Times responds, "That's a good question."[38] More poignantly, Dizzy asks another Minuteman (near the end of the series) what his story is, and he says, "How the hell do I know? I'm in it."[39]

With motives and controlling forces unclear, the ultimate anxiety of identity in contemporary culture is that there is no clear center, even when the "truth" is discovered. When Times does reawaken to his life as a Minuteman, he is "the Pointman," a stone cold killer, with a dead eye and the respect of other made men. Even though there is a certain cool appeal to his Minuteman incarnation, the character that he had played, with all of its quirky humor and insecurity, seemed to have more depth. As Ahrens states in his article on the series, "The irony is that—in a comment on the clichés of mass culture—the Minutemen are given clichés as personalities when they are truly themselves, whereas they appear as classic full characters when living in their brainwashed state."[40]

An interesting variation on this and perhaps the most disturbing take on the reawakening of the sleeper comes with Milo Garret, known among the Minutemen as "the Bastard" for his love of wanton violence. As Garret serves as the narrator of his own hardboiled detective story, he exits the hospital with his face completely bandaged. In addition to working as a private investigator (who in short order has a seductive and deceptive woman as his client), Garret's bandaged face is another cliché of crime fiction seen in classic and contemporary crime comics such as "Faced with Horror" in *Crime SuspenStories* and *Sin City: A Dame to Kill For*. Since everyone recognizes the man with bandaged face but no one knows the man beneath the bandages, the bandaged face makes identity simultaneously obvious and unknown.

Agent Graves informs Garret that it was no accident that led to his current state and leaves him with a 100-bullet briefcase and the opportunity to "get a piece of [himself] back."[41]

In short order, the briefcase and his new case have him embroiled in twisty pulp story involving a femme fatale, shady art dealers, a crime family, and another former enforcer for the family named Lono. More than any other Minuteman, Garret's cover story as a sleeper contains earmarks of genre fiction as evidenced by Garret's hardboiled narration: "I'd spent too much time–not to mention money–bettin' on ponies to believe in a sure thing. Not that the proof in the attaché didn't add up–it was all there, as plain as the nose that used to be on my face… But no why. No motive. No quinella. So no wonder I was thinkin' the gift horse had false teeth."[42] When Garret awakens from his sleep and remembers who he is, he provokes Lono to the point that Lono kills him. Repeating the opening monologue to himself as he dies, Garret has become more comfortable with the script of his classic crime story than the new, more brutal crime story of his "real" life: the story of *100 Bullets*.

Fig. 4.4
In his death throws, Garret desperately holds onto the fiction of his identity as a hard-boiled detective
100 Bullets No. 36, Vertigo, 2002
© Brian Azzarello, Eduardo Risso, and DC Comics

Although exploring noir themes in a meta-fictive way, the play of Azzarello's work is very serious and his humor terribly dark and made more so by the abstract representation in the artwork by Risso. Like Miller, he walks a line between realism and caricature with certain characters impossibly large and others cartoonish in their proportions. One of his consistent stylistic effects reveals the heart of the narrative separate from realistic considerations, such as the light source, wherein characters often become black silhouettes in the transition from one panel to the next. Sometimes the only detail left within the black silhouette is the white teeth of a sinister smile, and other times, in Azzarello's desire to show the consequences of violence, Risso covers the silhouettes in streams of red blood.

As the series proceeds, Risso demonstrates his ability to arrange panels on a page in order to show the overlap of various plot threads, very important as Agent Graves's end game plays out. The dissolution of the Minutemen is revealed to be a ruse orchestrated between Agent Graves and two other leaders of the thirteen crime families in order to consolidate power. The many pawns in play within Agent Graves's game begin to intersect, and their roles relative to one another become more apparent. However, this doesn't mean that Azzarello doesn't represent stories that Agent Graves doesn't directly influence, but often presents stories thematically related to the Minuteman stories.

MY MOUTH WAS A STEW OF PULP AND SPLINTERED TEETH BEFORE I REALIZED TOO LATE I'D BITTEN OFF MORE THAN I COULD CHEW...
...WHICH LEFT ME SPITTIN' DISTANCE FROM THE GRAVE.
I GOT ROOKED INTO BEING A PAWN IN A GAME I DIDN'T WANT TO PLAY, SO I CHEATED.
BUT YOU CAN'T CHEAT A CHEATER, AND THAT'S WHAT LIFE IS--THE DIRTIEST CHEATER OF ALL. SHE DON'T PLAY BY ANY ONE MAN'S RULES. NOT EVER...
...AND CERTAINLY NOT THIS NIGHT.
THIS MORNING, I WOKE UP IN A HOSPITAL.
"SO MR. GARRET, HOW YOU FEELIN'?" THE DOC SAYS.
"NUMB," I SAY BACK.
HE CHUCKLES A BIT, TELLS ME YOU CAN'T FEEL NUMB, 'CAUSE NUMB MEANS YOU CAN'T FEEL.
YOU CAN'T FEEL NUMB, YOU CAN ONLY BE NUMB, HE TELLS ME.

GUESS YOU FUCKED THAT, HUH?
I'D SAY YOU FUCKED IT ROYAL.
WALK.
I'D SAY SO.
NO.
NO MORE WALKIN', LOOP...
RUN.
BAM

Fig. 4.5
Jack Daw, "the Monster," becomes a dark silhouette not through backlighting but through a change in character
100 Bullets No. 92, Vertigo, 2008

In "A Crash," Graves's negotiations with the crime families is intercut with the story of a young couple that investigates a car crash to find a dead man with a winning lottery ticket in his hand. The couple plans to steal the ticket and give some of the money to his family, but the responding police officers take it from them and pocket it for themselves. The end of their story is narrated by the words one of the family leaders offers to Agent Graves as they look over the city: "Tiny lives. Listen closely, you can hear them... gasping for breath. They share the same air. But nothing else. Big hopes. Bigger disappointments."[43] In the world of *100 Bullets*, it might not be as accurate to say that God is indifferent and absent as to say God is merciless and allows the violence of evil men to undo them and those near them. After revealing the secret history of the Minutemen, the Minuteman named Victor Ray finishes an utterance by one of his dying crew who says, "Victor... Jesus..." "Is never around when you need him."[44] When Times tries to rescue a small-time virtuoso trumpet player, he discovers the musician's jaw has been severed in a bear trap and his criticism of the divine order is much more direct: "Oh fuck. Oh God. Fuck you."[45]

Agent Graves, who played God in the lives of many, claims not to believe in God,[46] but this does not exempt him from the violent retribution of the order of things. With the claim of the last standing member of the crime families that "the choice is always there,"[47] Agent Graves's plans fall apart and nearly all members of the thirteen families' leadership and the Minutemen (including Agent Graves) die due to situations created by their own guilt. And in the end, the 100-bullet briefcase moves from being an ostensible gimmick to a metaphor for the mechanics of those made powerful by their own maliciousness in modern civilization.

Although pushing the boundaries of mainstream acceptability with content typical of contemporary crime comics like *Sin City*, Azzarello more clearly articulates his position against the dehumanizing effect of violence. This is significant as he made a move like Brian Michael Bendis; writing some superhero comic books during the long run of *100 Bullets*, he pushes superheroes, a genre predicated on the justifiable exercise of violence, toward crime fiction even more extremely than his notable predecessors. In a way that comically harkens to the words of Fredric Wertham, Azzarello states, "Pretty much every comic is a crime comic, you know? Just because he wears a cape and has an 'S' on his chest doesn't mean he's not a cop, you know? And the Joker's a criminal."[48] And with those superhero stories, he managed to inject his dark take on the superhero mythology, rejecting the heroic god-man paradigm and righteous violence generally associated with the superhero.

While he worked with major superhero properties like Superman and Batman, Azzarello became most notable (and controversial) for his reworkings of villains and antiheroes in the DC and Marvel universe. In the limited series *Lex Luthor, Man of Steel* (2005), the story is narrated by Luthor who is completely justified in his crusade against Superman, portrayed in Lee Bemejo's artwork as a dark, red-eyed threat to humankind. In *Joker* (2008), a graphic novel coinciding with Christopher Nolan's *The Dark Knight* film, the Joker is extreme and unbalanced as usual but his tale works within the framework of a crime story. Retrieved by a low-level gang member when he is released from Arkham Asylum, the Joker goes on a killing spree to reclaim his territory and his reputation on the streets that were lost when other Batman criminals like the Penguin and Two-Face gained status in his absence. Working not just against Batman but against the vicious natural law of Gotham City's mean streets, the Joker takes shape as the ultimate crime lord for Gotham City.

In reference to these stories, Azzarello explains the essence of these characterizations, "What's the trick to writing a good bad guy? Well, for me, it's always been the idea that you pit yourself against authority."[49] And this is central to his earlier, more controversial treatment of Luke Cage, in the Marvel MAX series *Cage* (2002), rejected by the fans of the superhero because the morally ambiguous protagonist may have had a great street rep and no real superpowers. Although the series begins with the hero for hire seeming to take on a virtuous case with no money attached, he ultimately becomes more interested in pitting gangs against each other for his own gain. Seeming to recommend a gangsta thug as the closest thing to a hero in his fallen world, *Cage* draws much more heavily on the social criticism and exploitation aspects of the Blaxploitation films that inspired but never really shaped *Luke Cage, Power Man* in the 1970s. Like Bendis, Azzarello relies on the reader's previous knowledge of superhero stories to form a meta-discourse that undermines traditional superheroic tropes. In the case of *Cage*, Azzarello reveals not only heroism but also the power claimed by those who put themselves in positions of authority to be a sham.

Loving the Lowlife: Ed Brubaker's Superheroes and Vigilantes

Like Bendis, Ed Brubaker furthered his exposure to the world of comic books by working in comic book stores, thrilling to the seemingly endless possibilities promised by the direct market before the bust of the early 1990s.[50] Unlike Bendis and Azzarello, Brubaker didn't have an obvious early commitment to crime fiction, initially drawn to the mode of autobiographical realism practiced by Harvey Peker and Chester Brown and favored by *The Comics Journal*.[51]

However, *Lowlife*, his first major work published by Slave Labor Graphics, utilized an increasingly dark and detached sense of humor throughout the series. Loosely autobiographical, *Lowlife* explored the protagonist's trouble with drugs and girls, a result of his efforts to escape the banality of his life. Drawn by Brubaker with clean lines and a caricatured, cartoon-like style, *Lowlife* nevertheless often places its characters within the tight confines of highly detailed cityscapes. Although *Lowlife* could never be comfortably categorized as a crime comic, it nevertheless shows interests that relate to crime comics and would drive his career.

Brubaker began writing crime stories for the Dark Horse anthology, *Dark Horse Presents*, in 1991 (the first showcase and year of debut for *Sin City*). With stories like "An Accidental Death" and "The Fall," Brubaker demonstrated his interest in "lowlife" criminals and simple situations spinning out of control. Despite his initial leaning toward art comics, Brubaker admits, "I was never one of those people who dismissed genre stuff. I dismissed mysteries because it seemed stupid to read stuff with a solution at the end, like a crossword puzzle, until I actually read some good ones, like Hammet and Chandler."[52] In comics, he identified Johnny Craig's work with mysteries and EC as some of his favorites.[53]

With his moves from Slave Labor to Caliber to Dark Horse, Brubaker progressively worked his way toward mainstream publishers and was published by Vertigo in 1995 with a trippy revival of a Joe Simon creation, *Prez: Smells Like Teen President*. Much more significantly, this would lead to *Scene of the Crime*, a limited series that paired Brubaker with his future partners in crime, illustrators Michael Lark and Sean Phillips, whose realistic but moody styles owed much to classic film noir. With Jack Herriman as a private investigator on the trail of a client's missing sister, the series owes quite a bit to classic, hardboiled detective fiction. However, Brubaker updates it with Herriman's investigation leading to the workings of a commune and makes it a self-conscious treatment of the genre. Herriman runs his office from an art gallery that belongs to and exhibits the work of his uncle, a famous crime scene photographer who uses his celebrity to help Herriman. With this dynamic in place, Brubaker implicitly explores the idea of crime as fetish and the way that the violence of real life might be aestheticized via a particular perspective.

Although none of his work was phenomenally popular, Brubaker signed a short-term exclusive contract with DC Comics and began work with superhero characters who had significant crime comic connections: Batman and Catwoman. During this period, Brubaker would share much in common with Bendis's work from the same period: *Powers* and *Alias*. With his 2001 revision of *Catwoman*, Brubaker transformed an approach that passed off a gratuitous, cheesecake presentation of the Catwoman as "adult" to one that developed her as a genuinely complex, morally ambiguous crime character.

Although clearly placing the characters in a modern setting, Brubaker harkened to the pulp source material of early comics in a distinctive choice of supporting characters: Slam Bradley, the private investigator first produced by the creators of *Superman* Jerry Siegel and Joe Shuster. The series was illustrated by Darwyn Cooke, former storyboard artist for Bruce Tim's *Batman: The Animated Series*, a television show that emphasized a dark, art deco version of Gotham. With a style similar to that of Michael Avon Oeming, Cooke evokes *Dick Tracy* but synthesizes Chester Gould with Harvey Kurtzman and presents seedy content beyond the scope of the comic strip detective. In fact, it was thanks to the success of Bendis and Avon Oeming's *Powers* (as well as Brubaker's success with *Catwoman*) that Brubaker was able to move forward a series conceived with fellow writer Greg Rucka: *Gotham Central*, an Ed McBain-style police procedural set in Gotham City. With illustration by Michael Lark emphasizing a sense of urban decay, *Gotham Central* followed the work of beat cops clearly out of their depth with investigations often leading to supervillains they can't catch. Brubaker states, their situation "has to be completely demoralizing. They have to hate the fact that their commissioner has given them a time limit to catch the guy before he turns on the Bat Signal and brings in the big guns… It's about these characters that are the last good cops in a city working in an environment that none can quite fathom."[54]

In contrast to Bendis's work on *Alias*, Brubaker and Rucka don't use the crime story as a means to deconstruct the superhero story so much as to use the superhero story as a means extend the alienated psychology that drives the crime story. Marcus Driver, the detective who lost his partner to Mr. Freeze, is informed in quick succession that Batman has caught Mr. Freeze and that a child in a kidnapping case has been found murdered. He says, "Damn it all to hell," at which point he looks over and sees Batman standing nearby and adds, "and damn you too."[55] Typically portrayed as a violent outsider, *Gotham Central* makes Batman into a character who the detectives question, mistrust, and resent because his successes belittle their meager attempts to make things right. Brubaker ambitiously takes the most clearly noir superhero and makes him part of the establishment that oppresses the ordinary man–a commentary on the post-Wertham superhero. And Brubaker and Rucka made other moves with series that push them clearly into neo-noir content such as outing Gotham City detective Renee Montoya as a lesbian.

Loving Dr. Wertham and the Lowlife in Family-Friendly Comics: Ed Brubaker's *Criminal*

While working on *Gotham Central*, Brubaker did more superhero work with the Wildstorm series *Sleeper*, but more famously he began work with Marvel and *Captain America* in 2005–leading to the famous (albeit temporary) death of Captain America. In a now-typical superhero rite of passage for a crime comics writer, Brubaker developed an arc for *Daredevil* that lasted between 2006 and 2009. He began with a story point left by Bendis nearly impossible to follow in a superhero world without being unfair and denying the natural development of the storyline. Daredevil's civilian identity had been revealed to the public, and he is imprisoned for his life as a vigilante. Brubaker not only writes a prison drama that explores the psychology of those on the inside (now including Daredevil) but eventually writes Daredevil out of his superficial illusion that he can ever resume his life as Matt Murdock, lawyer. Moving beyond the secret identity and confronting the darkness within has become the *Daredevil* project passed from Miller to Bendis to Brubaker. Regardless, Brubaker's time at Marvel led to the most mainstream presentation of a straightforward story of a crime comic in contemporary comics publishing.

Published by Marvel's Icon but proudly labeled as a Marvel publication in trade paperback collections, *Criminal* began in 2006 as a run of short series like *Sin City* in basic concept (as stories in a related crime world–Center City–and not necessarily presented in chronological order). With an overarching sense of the arbitrariness of events in the life of small-time criminals, Criminal creates an atmosphere of existential dread characteristic of crime fiction. Brubaker states, "I feel like the plots are almost secondary to the characters we've been creating, and the world, and even the mood. That's the thing I always liked best about Jim Thompson, James M. Cain, or David Goodis."[56] Working with Sean Phillips (the inker on *Scene of the Crime*), this mood is evoked with a visual homage to the first page of Johnny Craig's *Crime SuspenStory* "Dead Ringer"; a man begs for his life at the bottom of a splash page largely filled with a cold and unresponsive night sky on the first page of *Criminal*'s "Second Chance in Hell" arc.[57]

IF YOU WANT TO UNDERSTAND THE TRUTH ABOUT ANYONE, ABOUT WHO THEY ARE AND WHERE THEY CAME FROM AND WHAT THEY MIGHT DO, GOOD OR BAD... YOU HAVE TO LOOK BACK.
FIND THOSE MOMENTS WHERE TIME AND LIFE COLLIDED AND MADE A MARK THAT WON'T EVER GO AWAY.
LIKE BACK IN 1954, WHEN MY FATHER TOOK WALTER HYDE OUT TO A FIELD TO BREAK HIS KNEES AND PUT A BULLET THROUGH HIS LEFT EYE.
WAIT! JUST STOP - LISTEN TO ME!
PLEASE! JUST LET ME TALK!

Fig. 4.6
Homage is paid to first page of *Crime SuspenStories'* "Dead Ringer" *Criminal: The Dead and the Dying*, Marvel, 2008 © Ed Brubaker and Basement Gang, Inc.

The first story in the *Criminal* series is "Coward," with the title describing Leo Patterson, a professional thief who works jobs carefully so that he isn't caught or killed. With the self-protective nature of a con-man, Patterson gains the reputation of being a coward and admits to his fears in his narration of the story:

> A punk/pimp/gangsta/lowrider with a gun...
> Those idiots are canon-fodder for the system. But someone who follows the rules, who understands how to stay safe... will never rot to death in a 4 x 5 cement room. Sometimes I tell people about the rules and they ask what I'm so scared of... and I tell them. I'm scared of ending up like my father. Scared of dying where I most likely belong... in prison. But the way I see it... if you aren't scared in our line of work, then you just aren't thinking.[58]

Patterson understands the system and his fear of it shapes him into a cautious criminal, but that doesn't protect him from pain, like caring for his mentor with Alzheimer's and dealing with the aftermath of jobs gone tragically wrong. Brubaker describes Patterson's story as one in which the self-conscious protagonist tries to keep himself from a typical noir path, but the irresistible force of his life pushes him in this direction. "But his story, while subverting some of the noir conventions, still goes right to the main themes of good noir, which is the darkness and violence that exists inside us, and what we really fear. And that's kind of what I want to do with the book, to twist clichés of the genre in different and more interesting directions."[59] With skillful shadow play, Phillips reveals the darkness within Patterson and the fracturing of Patterson's psyche by dividing a single shadowy image of Patterson into multiple panels. Ironically, Patterson doesn't fear violence, but he knows it's not smart and only gives into his violent impulses when his mentor and his lover/partner-in-crime are killed in a double cross. Enacting revenge by killing those responsible for the double cross, he plans to die in the shooting but instead lies bleeding until the police come to arrest him: one of his worst fears realized.

"Lawless," the second story arc, focuses on Tracy Lawless, a damaged veteran who goes AWOL to avenge the death of his brother, a small-time criminal. Posing as a small-timer himself, he infiltrates the band of thieves of which his brother had been part in order to uncover the killer but falls for Mallory, his brother's lover, in the process. Due to the complicated and unexpected ending of the group's theft, Lawless agrees to work for the criminal for whom they stole. His agreement means he can protect Mallory (who now hates him) and that he must follow in the path laid out by his father and brother (a criminal path that he once thought didn't need to be his own). And so it often goes in the stories in *Criminal*, with virtue often punished in a culture designed to favor the ruthless, violent, and rich.

This critique of an unjust system is furthered in "Bad Night," a story that charts a course to Brubaker's overtly meta-textual work, *The Last of the Innocent*. From the start of the series with "Coward," Brubaker featured a comic strip in the Center City newspaper called *Frank Kafka*, about a tough private eye, drawn with clean lines in the style of *Dick Tracy*. However, with the character's name alluding to the grueling social critique and fatalism of Franz Kafka, the strip is more than a *Dick Tracy* imitation intended as an ironic contrast to the stark "reality" of Center City.

In "Bad Night," Jacob Kurtz is a forger who gave up his criminal life to work on the strip but is blackmailed back into his criminal life by a femme fatale. As the story proceeds, it becomes apparent that Frank Kafka exists on several levels. Within the comic strip, Kurtz parodies a police officer who dogged him in the past, and the humiliation of the officer drives him to corruption and revenge against Kurtz. With the strip as both a catharsis and a self-condemnation (commenting on reality and making reality), the strip is revealed as part of Kurtz's life in more profound ways; he literally interacts with the two-dimensional Frank Kafka, a character artistically out of synch with the grainy realism of the rest of Kurtz's world. A darkly humorous counterpoint to Kurtz's life as it spirals out of control, Frank Kafka's hard advice and presence in Kurtz's life becomes just as dreadful as everything else. In the end, it is revealed that the character became part of his life when Kurtz first committed murder and wasn't caught but now leaves him as Kurtz commits murder again and is caught.

In many ways, this work is a prologue for Brubaker's *Criminal: The Last of the Innocent*, a title that he identifies as a riff on *Seduction of the Innocent*.[60] The story begins with Riley Richards as a man made desperate by gambling debts while he works for the rich and hateful father of the wife who cheats on him with his high school rival; this life is represented in Philips's trademark style for the series, a naturalistic representation of a decaying urban setting exaggerated to some degree by an expressionist sense of light and darkness and some interesting monochromatic compositions. Drawn back to the small town of his youth by his father's life-threatening sickness (and then death), Richards begins to think nostalgically about his youth and Lizzie Gordon, the cute girl next door whom he left for his rich wife. This look into that past from his perspective is rendered in a style of art like that of *Archie* comics, with the protagonist as Archie, the girl next door as Betty, and so on. "I made the decision to show all the flashbacks in a kids comic style. It's part of the larger theme, too, of showing these innocent kids growing into Dr. Wertham's nightmares of what kids in the '50s would turn into."[61] Curiously, these flashbacks present the scenes in artwork associated with the teen humor comics that epitomized what would be safe for youth, and yet the content of the scenes is anything but sanitized. Revealing the underbelly of his young life (Richards's teenage sex with his future wife; his young best friend's abuse of drugs; and serial killing used to cover up a calculated small-town murder), Richards nevertheless idealizes these simply rendered and brilliantly colored memories: "I see all the lazy Sundays in the world. And I have this strange feeling… that I can go back and fix all the mistakes I made… And that's when I know. I know how to get it all back… how to escape… I have to kill my wife."[62]

Fig. 4.7
Through a standard convention of crime comics representation, Leo Patterson is divided over two panels *Criminal: Coward*, Marvel, 2006 © Ed Brubaker and Basement Gang, Inc.

He launches his plan to reclaim his happiness by killing his wife and provides himself an alibi by going on a binge with his now clean best friend, Freakout. Despite the suspicions of his father-in-law and the danger Freakout presents as an alibi, Richards manages to outsmart his father-in-law and remove Freakout as a problem with a convenient drug overdose. As Richards gets away with murder and begins to live his life with the girl next door, the artistic style representing the present slowly morphs into the *Archie* comics style of his past as he narrates, "It feels like a new beginning... Like I'm finally safe. Because the last person—maybe the only person—who really knew me [Freakout]... is lying on the slab in the Brookview county morgue. So now I can be whoever I want."[63] Finding joy in one of the ultimate anxieties in crime fiction (the loss of an authentic self), Brubaker critiques the false security that might be found in comic books that are identified as safe for youth. Concomitantly, the title provides much room for interpretive play and arguably may be a tragic lamentation, referring to the generation before Richards or to Freakout. However, when regarding the work as a whole, the best argument seems to be for it as a reference to Richards himself, thus making problematic the notion of pure innocence.

Fig. 4.8
Riley Richards' world transforms from a rendering in gritty realism of comics noir into the cartoony style of *Archie* comics
Criminal: The Last of the Innocent, Marvel, 2011 © Ed Brubaker and Basement Gang, Inc.

Bendis, Azzarello, and Brubaker all take crime comics seriously while at the same time they analyze the tropes of crime fiction and the comics medium in self-conscious and perhaps postmodern ways. All find corruption at the source and deny the myth of the innocent past in superhero comics, teen humor comics, and what comics in part represent—U.S. history. Regardless, *The Last of the Innocent* may be the most finely tuned as both an embodiment and analysis of the crime comics aesthetic in that Brubaker not only rewrites teen comedy comics with crime fiction, he demonstrates the way that human experience is always mediated in contemporary culture and based on one's media of choice (media that might conceal or reveal the dirty underbelly of contemporary culture). He does so by bringing together impulses drawn from the beginning of his career and characteristic of his work on *Criminal*. In reference to a narrative convention typical in crime fiction and used extensively in *Criminal*, Brubaker states, "I found the first-person narrative in detective fiction feels almost like the first person narrative in autobiography."[64] In addition, he furthers this idea with a specific reference to *The Last of the Innocent*: "I was surprised... that it was more personal than the shit I did when I was doing loose autobiography. I'm writing about stuff that means more to me, I think, than the stuff I was writing about in *Lowlife*."[65]

THE NEXT DAY, BROCK CALLS TO TELL ME FREAKOUT HAS DIED OF AN OVERDOSE.
HE DOESN'T SOUND VERY SURPRISED.
SURE... THANKS... YOU TOO.
EVERYTHING OKAY?
OH YEAH... JUST MY MOM.
I DECIDE IT'S BEST TO NOT TELL LIZZIE RIGHT AWAY.
THINGS ARE GOING SO WELL...
LET US HAVE A BIT MORE SUN AND FUN BEFORE THE CLOUDS COME BACK.
SHE'LL UNDERSTAND.
SHE ALWAYS DOES.
SO WHAT'S ON THE AGENDA TODAY?
I DON'T KNOW... HOW ABOUT WE TRY THAT NEW BRUNCH PLACE?

THERE'S A DULL PAIN IN MY STOMACH. A HEARTSICKNESS, I GUESS.
BUT IT FEELS LIKE A NEW BEGINNING, TOO.
LIKE I'M FINALLY SAFE.
BECAUSE THE LAST PERSON -- MAYBE THE ONLY PERSON -- WHO REALLY KNEW ME...
...IS LYING ON A SLAB IN THE BROOKVIEW COUNTY MORGUE.
SO NOW I CAN BE WHOEVER I WANT.
THE END
Brubaker Phillips

Although crime fiction has been criticized as an overly stylized and skewed representation of reality, it seems for Brubaker that crime fiction provides the best way to represent the inevitably biased and often tragic truths of his own experience in contemporary culture. And his perspective (albeit personal) brings us to the larger question of how we should understand the popular revival of crime comics that explore the desperation of contemporary culture through a dialogue with and reworking of the past of one's life, comic books, and the United States.

Fig. 4.9
Riley Richards' world transforms from a rendering in gritty realism of comics noir into the cartoony style of *Archie* comics
Criminal: The Last of the Innocent, Marvel, 2011 © Ed Brubaker and Basement Gang, Inc

Chapter 4 Notes

1 Keith Phipps, "Interview: Brian Michael Bendis," *The Onion*, last modified August 9, 2007, http://www.avclub.com/articles/brian-michael-bendis,14138/.

2 Ethan Sacks, "*100 Bullets*, Brian Azzarello and Eduardo Risso's Acclaimed Crime Comic Series, Ends with a Bang," *The New York Daily News*, last modified April 15, 2009, http://articles.nydailynews.com/2009-04-15/entertainment/17920871_1_comic-books-super-heroes-vertigo-comics.

3 Oliver Sava, "Interview: Ed Brubaker," *The Onion*, last modified July 20, 2011, http://www.avclub.com/articles/ed-brubaker,59143/.

4 Randy Duncan and Matthew Smith, *The Power of Comics: History, Form, and Culture* (New York: Continuum, 2009), 76; Jean-Paul Gabilliet, *Of Comics and Men: A Cultural History of American Comic Books*, trans. Bart Beatty and Nick Nguyen (Jackson: University of Mississippi Press, 2010), 156.

5 Duncan and Smith, *The Power of Comics*, 81.

6 Ronald Schwartz, *Neo-Noir: The New Film Noir Style from Psycho to Collateral* (Lanham, Maryland: The Scarecrow Press, 2005), xi.

7 Foster Hirsh, *Detours and Lost Highways: A Map of Neo-Noir* (New York: Limelight, 1999), 7.

8 Woody Haut, *Pulp Culture* (London: Serpent's Tail, 1996), 71–72.

9 Hirsh, *Detours and Lost Highways*, 12.

10 *City of Glass* was adapted as graphic novel, illustrated by David Mazzucchelli (who illustrated *Daredevil: Reborn* and *Batman: Year One*).

11 Paul Monaco, *John Dahl and Neo-Noir: Examining Auteurism and Genre* (Lanham, MD: Lexington, 2010), 41.

12 Rob M. Worley, "Max Allan Collins Brings 'Ms. Tree' to Novels and TV," *Mania*, last modified January 24, 2008, http://www.mania.com/max-allan-collins-brings-ms-tree-to-novels-tv_article_90640.html.

13 Arune Singh, "Just the Facts Ma'am: Max Collins Talks Road to Perdition," *Comic Book Resources*, last modified June 16, 2002, http://www.comicbookresourcescom/?page=article&id=1193.

14 Max Allan Collins and Terry Beatty, *Ms. Tree* (New York: PaperJacks, 1988), viii.

15 Ibid.

16 Hans Berten and Theo D'Haen, *Contemporary American Crime Fiction* (New York: Palgrave, 2001), 15.

17 Michael Dean, "The Brian Michael Bendis Interview," *The Comics Journal* 266 (Feb./Mar. 2005): 110, 104.

18 Phipps, "Interview: Brian Michael Bendis."

19 Brian Michael Bendis, *Goldfish* (Orange, CA: Image Comics, 2001), 54.

20 Michael Dean, "The Brian Michael Bendis Interview," 107.

21 Paul Morton, "An Interview with Brian Michael Bendis," *Bookslut*, last modified February 2009, http://www.bookslut.com/features/2009_02_014023.php.

22 Bendis, *Goldfish*, 247–248.

23 Brian Michael Bendis, *Jinx* (Orange, CA: Image Comics, 2001), 245.

24 Hirsh, *Detours and Lost Highways*, 278.

25 Dean, "The Brian Michael Bendis Interview," 95.

26 Marvel's Ultimate titles were launched in 2000 with *Ultimate Spider-Man* written by Bendis; *Ultimate X-Men*, *Ultimate Fantastic Four*, and others were quick to follow. The Ultimate titles were originally identified by Marvel as an attempt to retell stories of their characters for new readers without the burden of decades of continuity. Now, the Ultimate universe now has a great deal of its own convoluted continuity, requires significant background knowledge to fully understand, and no longer serves as a good introduction to Marvel characters for new readers.

27 Ibid., 113.

28 Brian Michael Bendis and Michael Gaydos, *Alias* (New York: Marvel Comics, 2003), 12. This is one of the most controversial parts of the series due largely to its portrayal of Luke Cage as a sexual opportunist. In Paul Morton, "An Interview with Brian Michael Bendis," Bendis states, "It is interesting that that element of it still stirs in some people. It's why the book was not printed at its original printer which was shocking to us as well... I absolutely have known people who continue to [punish themselves with sex]. And I wanted to write about it. And I am shocked I get to write about it in a Marvel comic book."

29 Brian Michael Bendis, *Alias: The Secret Origins of Jessica Jones* (New York: Marvel Comics, 2004), 120.

30 Ibid., 124.

31 Eric Evans, "*100 Bullets*: Axel Alonso, Brian Azzarello, Dave Johnson, Eduardo Risso," *The Comics Journal* 228 (October 2000): 93.

32 Ibid., 96.

33 Christopher Irving, "Brian Azzarello on Crime and Superheroes," *Graphic NYC*, last modified October 26, 2011, http://www.nycgraphicnovelists.com/2011/10/brian-azzarello-on-crime-and.html.

34 Evans, "*100 Bullets*," 93.

35 Brian Azzarello and Eduardo Risso, *100 Bullets: First Shot, Last Call* (New York: DC Comics, 1999), 17.

36 Ibid., 31.

37 Ibid., 72.

38 Brian Azzarello and Eduardo Risso, *100 Bullets: A Foregone Tomorrow* (New York: DC Comics, 2002), 215.

39 Brian Azzarello and Eduardo Risso, *100 Bullets: Wilt* (New York: DC Comics, 2009), 136.

40 Jorn Ahrens, "The Ordinary Urban: *100 Bullets* and the Clichés of Mass Culture," *Comics and the City: Urban Space in Print, Picture, and Sequence*, ed. Jorn Ahrens and Arno Meteling (New York: Continuum, 2010), 218–219. In "*Reservoir Dogs*: Redemption in a Postmodern World," Mark T. Conard offers an interesting similarity in Tarantino's neo-noir *Pulp Fiction*, wherein authentic "real people" are revealed to not be morally superior to clichéd "gangsters"; however, in a world where "violence is eroticized and stylized," gangster would most often be the role of choice. Mark T. Conard, "*Reservoir Dogs*: Redemption in a Postmodern World," *The Philosophy of Neo-Noir*, ed., Mark T. Conard (Lexington: University Press of Kentucky, 2007), 113.

41 Brian Azzarello and Eduardo Risso, *100 Bullets: The Counterfifth Detective* (New York: DC Comics, 2003), 24.

42 Ibid., 25.

43 Brian Azzarello and Eduardo Risso, *100 Bullets: Six Feet Under the Gun* (New York: DC Comics, 2003.), 117–118.

44 Brian Azzarello and Eduardo Risso, *100 Bullets: The Hard Way* (New York: DC Comics, 2005), 34.

45 Ibid., 151.

46 Azzarello and Risso, *100 Bullets: Wilt*, 283.

47 Ibid., 293.

48 Eric Evans, "*100 Bullets*," 96. In a similar quote that links superhero stories to hard-boiled detective fiction, Azzarello states, "I've always treated the cape as a trenchcoat." Irving, "Brian Azzarello on Crime and Superheroes."

49 Steve Ekstrom, "Exploring the Joker: Brian Azzarello Talks," *Newsarama*, last modified October 2, 2008, http://www.newsarama.com/comics/090802-AzzarelloJoker.html.

50 Tom Spurgeon, "The Ed Brubaker Interview," *The Comics Journal* 263 (October–November, 2004): 62.

51 Ibid., 63.

52 Ibid., 73.

53 Ibid., 77.

54 Ibid., 91.

55 Ed Brubaker, Greg Rucka, and Michael Lark, *Gotham Central: In the Line of Duty* (New York: DC Comics, 2012), 51.

56 Spurgeon, Tom, "A Short Interview with Ed Brubaker," *The Comics Reporter*, last modified August 26, 2006,http://www.comicsreporter.com/index.php/resources/interviews/5964/.

57 The visual allusions don't end there, with Teeg Lawless, a small time thief, wearing a bandage over his nose in *Criminal*'s "A Wolf among Wolves" arc like the protagonist in the neo-noir film *Chinatown*. Another intended but not fully realized EC comics connection is described by Brubaker in his overview of *The Last of the Innocent*; the depiction of the best-friend drug addict was intended to allude to the drug addict on the Al Feldstein cover of *Shock SuspenStories* No. 12 (Spurgeon, Tom, "CR Sunday Interview: Ed Brubaker," *The Comics Reporter*, last modified June 6, 2011, http://www.comicsreporter.com/index.php/cr_sunday_interview_ed_brubaker2012summer/).

58 Ed Brubaker and Sean Phillips, *Criminal: Coward* (New York: Marvel Comics, 2007), 4.

59 Spurgeon, "A Short Interview with Ed Brubaker."

60 Spurgeon, "CR Sunday Interview: Ed Brubaker."

61 Alex Zalben, "Interview: Ed Brubaker Tells Us Why the New *Criminal* Is the 'Ultimate Crime Comic,'" *MTV.com*, last modified June 1, 2011, http://geek-news.mtv.com/2011/06/01/interview-ed-brubaker-tells-us-why-the-new-criminal-is-the-ultimate-crime-comic/.

62 Brubaker, Ed, *Criminal: The Last of the Innocent* (New York: Marvel Comics, 2011), 24–25.

63 Ibid., 103.

64 Spurgeon, "The Ed Brubaker Interview," 77.

65 Spurgeon, "CR Sunday Interview: Ed Brubaker." An interesting connection between Brubaker's early interests in art comics and in the content of *The Last of the Innocent* is represented by the following: "I always dug *Archie* comics. That's one of the things about *Love and Rockets* that really appealed to me, too. How much it was like *Archie* comics for adults." Spurgeon, "The Ed Brubaker Interview," 66.

IT'S NOT ING BUT PAN ERING, CLICHE-R DDEN, GENRE C AP!
GAKK!
YOU'VE OT EVERY R HT TO YOUR DINION, PAL.

CONCLUSION

Crime Comics and America's Memento Mori

You know something? You read too many comic books.
James Dean as Jim Stark[1]

In the System: A Rebel with a Cause

Even though Fredric Wertham's ideas received too much credit from the general public during the congressional hearings of 1954, they received criticism almost immediately from people inside and outside the comic book industry. One of these more notable criticisms came from another medium: Nicholas Ray's *Rebel without a Cause*, a melodrama with crime fiction elements, released in 1955. When Jim, the teen protagonist, is being bullied by Buzz, the juvenile delinquent thug, Jim tells him he reads too many comic books (a line delivered deadpan by James Dean to indicate its sarcasm). At the end of *Seduction of the Innocent*, Wertham recounts his consolation of a distressed mother of a juvenile delinquent, clearly reiterating that the situation is not her fault. While not absolving media culture or youth, *Rebel without a Cause* moves in another direction, placing blame on parents–traditional authority figures who, in the film, have no moral high ground or certainty.

Despite the lack of esteem given to Wertham even at that time (a lack that has grown over time), I must admit that Wertham was right. Not about youth psychology and culture (something that he misunderstood and feared). And not in that comics were for children (and could be made safe by removing sex and violence). But in that crime comics promote delinquency (not only for juveniles but also for adults). Of course, delinquency (criminally offensive behavior) is always something narrowly defined by the powers-that-be who find thinking outside terms they define as being criminally offensive. I believe this study works very effectively to demonstrate this as an intentional goal of contemporary creators of comics noir and practitioners of the comic noir style. This applies even and perhaps especially to creators who are part of the second generation of the resurgence of crime comics, questioning the genre in order to leave nothing untouched by their general questioning of the status quo.

Crime comics offer a much less optimistic view than that presented by people invested in morally questionable benefits of industrial and post-industrial culture; crime comics offer a nuanced criticism of society that can never be appreciated by those who see thoughtful questions and criticism as un-American activity.

The comic noir creators whose work I have profiled offer criticism and questions about society but never promise answers to any social problems that they might identify. With that stated, these creators pose their criticisms and questions by crafting stories that depict individuals confronting the systemic problems of society. Motter, Chaykin, and Miller do this much more directly than Bendis, Azzarello, and Brubaker. Chaykin is the most idealistic, with Reuben Flagg, who tries to change the system and reawaken past ideals. For all his grittiness, Miller is not far behind as a moralist, although his hero's quests take place on smaller scales that allow their small successes to remain secret; Marv's quest to avenge Goldie puts to an end not the general evil but the specific evil represented by Cardinal Rourke. Heroes like John Hartigan fight for the fading idealism of the past in the rapid decay of Basin City represented in his fight for Nancy's innocence. As with Chaykin's heroes, Miller's heroes often discover that past ideal is nothing but a fiction, but they fight for it anyway. The faulty notion that the perfect past has been lost is critiqued even more by Motter with Mr. X, whose past and identity are uncertain, but he still feels he has so much work to do to reclaim his perfect past (futilely toiling with his industrial-age work ethic).

The second generation in the resurgence does not even allow their heroes (or readers) the fiction of a past ideal. *Alias* reveals the corruption at the source with superhero comics, *The Last of the Innocent* with *Archie* comics, and *100 Bullets* with the birth of the U.S. itself. However, in a fairly Godless world, the characters find redemption in small ways: Cage's semi-heroic start (if not end), Tracy Lawless's sacrifice (that still leaves him hated and indentured), and Goldfish and Jinx's relationship (that redeems his criminal life in a minor way but won't change the Goldfish's eventual failure of his son). And Jinx and Dizzy provide a redress to the man's world sexism of classic crime fiction but are characters who are ultimately just as likely to be condemned to a tragic end thanks to the world's general oppressiveness. Thus, we end with the two-part definition offered in the introduction: noir is a story of a crime that explores the desperation of industrial and post-industrial life through visual design that essentializes and distorts; and comic noir not only dialogues more openly with noir traditions of the past but also reworks noir with an aesthetic approach that reveals the conventions of the genre and the medium.

"So Much to Do, So Little Time": The Long Night

My goal was to identify distinctive stages of the comic noir resurgence as connected to crime fiction in other mediums as well as to numerous historical factors influencing the medium in particular and thought in general. My related secondary goal was to represent these stages through the work of the most important, influential, and self-conscious creators of comics noir. As a consequence, many comic noir creators have not been mentioned (or have been mentioned only in passing): Jason Aaron, Darwyn Cooke, Garth Ennis, David Lapham, Greg Rucka, Andrew Vachss, Brian K. Vaughn, John Wagner, and Matt Wagner, among others. Also, I chose to focus primarily on writer/artists and writers, but have tried to give the illustrators equal credit in creating noir worlds. And in connection to other crime fiction, I left out many classic authors and filmmakers and new wave crime authors and neo-noir filmmakers. These acknowledgements are made not to point out a weakness in my work but to highlight its selectivity and perhaps encourage continued work in this fertile area for research. Along these lines, I don't want to ignore that the creators I discussed continue to work beyond the eras profiled. Motter extends the mythology of Mr. X's world with stories of other cities of his dark antique future with *Terminal City, Electropolis*, and a reboot of Mr. X in *Mr. X: Condemned*. Chaykin continues to reject baseless nostalgia with works like *American Century* and *Avengers 1959* and defies the boundaries of good taste with a prequel to *Black Kiss*. Miller parodies his own work with *The Dark Knight Strikes Again* and *All Star Batman and Robin* and refines his political outsider status with the propagandistic *Holy Terror*. Also, Miller co-directs film adaptations of *Sin City*, influencing mainstream film with graphic content and green screen comic book-style imagery.[2] Max Allan Collins becomes even more closely associated with classic crime fiction with *Road to Perdition* and with new Mike Hammer novels based on Mickey Spillane's unfinished work. Bendis continues to integrate his gritty perspective into the world of mainstream superheroes as one of the most important architects of the Marvel universe with his work on the *Avengers* and seemingly innumerable cross-over events like *Secret Invasion*. Azzarello becomes the standard bearer for contemporary crime comics, producing *Filthy Rich* (the first graphic novel in the Vertigo Crime line) and brings together most great pulp heroes (Batman, Doc Savage, the Spirit, and more) in *First Wave*. And Brubaker (and Phillips) stretches the boundaries of noir further toward horror with *Fatale* and continues his run on *Criminal*.

Crime comics have once again become incredibly popular, and their publication is not threatened by purveyors of good taste or protectors of the American way; crime comics are unlikely to go away even though comic books have changed, and they may be marketed more often than before as graphic novels, e-texts, or webcomics. This situation begs the question of whether something this popular might be subversive: is the so-called outlaw really a sellout? It is important to mention that crime fiction in general and crime comics in particular were never unpopular; they appealed to working class readers and were largely rejected by those self-appointed few who sought to protect the standards of high art. This "protection" continues today in the pages of *The Comics Journal*, advocating for alternative neorealist comic art and only occasionally recommending mainstream genre material. Miller,[3] Bendis,[4] Brubaker,[5] and others have complained about this problematic position, and Jorn Ahrens comments on this position, represented by Kent Worcester in a *Comics Journal* review of *100 Bullets*:

Fig. Con.1
The Comics Journal
No. 209,
Fantagraphics, 1998
Marv strangles a radio talk show host (Ray Suarez from *Talk of the Nation*) for his critique of *Sin City*: the way Miller confront his critics and *The Comics Journal* acknowledges its own pretensions

> Following Worcester, one crucial characteristic of a comic that is of cultural relevance seems to be its documentary quality, or at least its appeal to realism... Ironically, when Worcester celebrates the staging of the "ordinary" as a merit in this medium, his clear-cut distinction between the broad field of mainstream comics (including those "a cut above the norm") and the predictable? limited rest—which were of cultural and academic relevance, since their quality was above the norm—sharply rejects the ordinary (as vulgar) in the aesthetic and narrative form of comics themselves.[6]

In addition to the contradiction within the argument of Worcester who seeks to disqualify *100 Bullets* and crime comics as art, Ahrens furthers his analysis of *100 Bullets* and effectively shows why comic noir remains subversive: "The allegation that a comic like *100 Bullets* is mainstream, and therefore irrelevant, is more than ineffective, since today mainstream-culture products define the very standard of cultural reflection and representation... By conjoining the self, violence, and urbanity, *100 Bullets* also finds its own historical and medial meta-representation that explicitly reflects its own ambiguities."[7] Contemporary comics noir may be even more subversive than classic crime comics due to their excessive self-awareness, subverting culture and upholding the genre while also subverting the genre. Comic noir lives up to expectations and then frustrates them and its frustration usually includes a frustration of the notion of self supplied by high culture.

IT'S NOTHING BUT PANDERING, CLICHE-RIDDEN, GENRE CRAP!
GAKK!
SNAP!
YOU'VE GOT EVERY RIGHT TO YOUR OPINION, PAL.

In *Byline: Mickey Spillane* (a collection of obscure Spillane material that traces Mike Hammer back to Spillane's comic book character, Mike Danger), Max Allan Collins describes Spillane's temporary, decade-long retirement from novel writing. Upon publishing *Kiss Me Deadly* (his eighth novel in five years), Spillane had become a household name and a fairly rich man. And yet, he spent the next decade publishing in low-end magazines, trying to find a comfortable place for his work that up to that point had been much maligned by the critics. Of course, this was not a move meant to endear him to the critics. "[H]e would encourage his publisher to advertise in the book trades with excerpts from the worst reviews placed next to the through-the-roof sales figures of each."[8] And Collins himself would elsewhere identify the best piece of advice that he received from Spillane: "Critics don't know anything; only the public knows."[9]

Regardless of the votes cast by critics for good or ill, the comic book reading public has cast its vote for the dark critique made by contemporary comics noir. The public has been curiously drawn into worlds with no clear answers, perhaps recognizing those worlds are something like the worlds readers inhabit. Comic noir has little hope for systemic change because in comic noir, human culture is an outgrowth of basic human nature (with that nature amplified via the congestion, rapidly outmoded technology, and unending urban decay of contemporary cities).

Hope cannot change human nature, but understanding may be able to improve human life in small ways by providing a better means of interacting with contemporary culture (limiting the vice of the powerful and giving integrity to the powerless). The title of this work is, of course, a play on Miller's most famous treatment of Batman and the change to Miller's title is meant to indicate that the grim and gritty superhero is only a small part of a much more important trend: the resurgence of crime comics. And with such a title, it's important to ask whether the night first clearly seen in classic crime comics actually went away. Certainly, its clear expression went underground when stamped out by a system threatened by the masses with their new literacies and raw frustrations. However, the feelings didn't go away, and they continued to develop as part of the multimedia dynamic that is crime fiction. And they will continue to develop in interesting and perhaps more startling ways thanks to the presence of contemporary comics noir, a dark night that has returned with no foreseeable end in sight.

Conclusion Notes

1 *Rebel without a Cause*, directed by Nicholas Ray (Burbank, CA: Warner Bros., 1955).

2 Miller co-directed *Sin City* with Robert Rodriguez at Rodriguez's insistence in order to better represent the visual style of the source material. Miller also received co-directing credit with Rodriguez. Prohibited by the Director's Guild of America, Rodriguez would lose his membership as a consequence. Rodriguez, a genre film director, set himself outside the system with this choice but it has had little detrimental effect on his career. (This relates to the point that crime stories have long been meant for the masses not interested in buying only what the system has to sell.) The success of *Sin City* led to Miller's first solo work as a screenwriter and director for *The Spirit*, another green screen production intended to translate the experience of graphic literature to film. However, Miller made Eisner's classic crime comic into an absurdist superhero story, and it was widely rejected by critics and fans.

3 Milo George, *Frank Miller: The Interviews: 1981–2003* Seattle: Fantagraphics, 2003), 118.

4 Michael Dean, "The Brian Michael Bendis Interview," *The Comics Journal* 266 (Feb./Mar. 2005): 126.

5 Tom Spurgeon, "The Ed Brubaker Interview," *The Comics Journal* 263 (October–November, 2004): 97.

6 Jorn Ahrens, "The Ordinary Urban: *100 Bullets* and the Clichés of Mass Culture," *Comics and the City: Urban Space in Print, Picture, and Sequence*, ed. Jorn Ahrens and Arno Meteling (New York: Continuum, 2010), 215.

7 Ibid., 227.

8 Max Allan Collins and Lynn F. Myers, "Introduction: I, the Writer," *Byline: Mickey Spillane*, ed. Max Allan Collins and Lynn F. Myers (Norfolk, VA: Crippen and Landru, 2004), 10.

9 A. Hudson, "Interview with Max Allan Collins," *Comic Attack*, last updated June 3, 2012, http://comicattack.net/2012/06/invmaxallancollins/.

Ahrens, Jorn. "The Ordinary Urban: *100 Bullets* and the Clichés of Mass Culture." *Comics and the City: Urban Space in Print, Picture, and Sequence*. Edited by Jorn Ahrens and Arno Meteling, 214–28. New York: Continuum, 2010.

Ahrens, Jorn and Arno Meteling, *Comics and the City: Urban Space in Print, Picture, and Sequence*. New York: Continuum, 2010.

Asch, Stan. "The Crystal Ball Killer." *War Against Crime* 2. New York: EC. June 1948.

Auster, Paul. *City of Glass*. New York: Penguin, [1985] 1987.

Azzarello, Brian and Lee Bermejo. *Joker*. New York: DC Comics, 2008.

——. *Luthor*. New York: DC Comics, 2010.

Azzarello, Brian and Richard Corben. *Cage*. New York: Marvel Comics, 2002.

Azzarello, Brian and Eduardo Risso. *100 Bullets: The Counterfifth Detective*. New York: DC Comics, 2003.

——. *100 Bullets: First Shot, Last Call*. New York: DC Comics, 1999.

——. *100 Bullets: A Foregone Tomorrow*. New York: DC Comics, 2002.

——. *100 Bullets: The Hard Way*. New York: DC Comics, 2005.

——. *100 Bullets: Six Feet Under the Gun*. New York: DC Comics, 2003.

——. *100 Bullets: Wilt*. New York: DC Comics, 2009.

——.*Jonny Double*. New York: DC Comics, 2002.

Bendis, Brian Michael. *Goldfish.* Orange, CA: Image Comics, 2001.

———. *Jinx.* Orange, CA: Image Comics, 2001.

Bendis, Brian Michael and Marc Andreyko. *Torso.* Orange, CA: Image Comics, 2000.

Bendis, Brian Michael and Mike Avon Oeming. *Powers,* Vol. 1. New York, Marvel Comics, 2005.

Bendis, Brian Michael and Michael Gaydos. *Alias.* New York: Marvel Comics, 2003.

———. *Alias: The Secret Origins of Jessica Jones.* New York: Marvel Comics, 2004.

———. *Alias: The Underneath.* New York: Marvel Comics, 2003.

Benton, Mike. *Crime Comics: The Illustrated History.* Dallas: Taylor Publishing, 1993.

Berten, Hans and Theo D'Haen. *Contemporary American Crime Fiction.* New York: Palgrave, 2001.

The Big Heat. Directed by Fritz Lang. Los Angeles: Columbia, 1953.

Black Widow. Directed by Nunnally Johnson. Los Angles: 20th Century Fox, 1954.

Blackmore, Tim. "Blind Daring: Vision and Revision in *Oedipus Tyrranus* and in Frank Miller's *Daredevil: Born Again.*" *Journal of Popular Culture* 27 (Winter 1993): 135–62.

———. "The Dark Knight of Democracy: Tocqueville and Miller Cast Some Light on the Subject." *Journal of American Culture* 14 (Spring 1991): 37–56.

Bloch, Ernst. *The Utopian Function of Art and Literature: Selected Essays.* Translated by Jack Zipes and Frank Mecklenburg. Cambridge: MIT, 1988.

Blood Simple. Directed by Joel Coen. Universal City, CA: Universal, 1984.

Body Double. Directed by Brian DePalma. Los Angeles: Columbia, 1984.

Borde, Raymond and Etienne Chaumeton. *A Panorama of American Film Noir: 1941–1953.* Translated by Paul Hammond. San Francisco: City Lights, 2002.

Bould, Mark, Kathrina Glitre, and Greg Tuck. *Neo-Noir*. London: Wallflower, 2009.

Brownstein, Charles. *Eisner/Miller*. Milwaukie, OR: Dark Horse, 2005.

Brubaker, Ed. *A Complete Lowlife*. Marietta, GA: Top Shelf, 2001.

Brubaker, Ed and Darwyn Cooke. *Catwoman: Trail of the Catwoman*. New York: DC Comics, 2012.

Brubaker, Ed and Michael Lark. *Daredevil: The Devil, Inside and Out*, Vol. 1. New York: Marvel Comics, 2006.

——. *Scene of the Crime*. New York: DC Comics, 2012.

Brubaker, Ed and Sean Phillips. *Criminal: Bad Night*. New York: Marvel Comics, 2009.

——. *Criminal*: Coward. New York: Marvel Comics, 2007.

——. *Criminal: The Dead and the Dying*. New York: Marvel Comics, 2008.

——. *Criminal: The Last of the Innocent*. New York: Marvel Comics, 2011.

——. *Criminal: Lawless*. New York: Marvel Comics, 2007.

Brubaker, Ed, Greg Rucka, and Michael Lark. *Gotham Central: In the Line of Duty*. New York: DC Comics, 2012.

Brubaker, Ed and Eric Shanower. *Prez: Smells Like Teen President*. New York: DC Comics, 1995.

Burnett, W.R. *Little Caesar*. Harpenden, UK: No Exit, [1929] 1989.

Cain, James. *Double Indemnity*. New York: Vintage, [1943] 1989.

Chandler, Raymond. *The Big Sleep*. New York: Vintage, [1939] 1988.

——. *The Simple Art of Murder*. New York: Vintage, [1950] 1988.

Chaykin, Howard. *American Flagg!* Berkeley, CA: Image Comics, 2008.

——. *Black Kiss.* Mt. Laurel, NJ: Dynamite, 2010.

——. *The Shadow: Blood and Judgment.* New York: DC Comics, 1987.

——. *Time2: The Epiphany.* Evanston, IL: First Comics, 1986.

——. *Time2: The Satisfaction of Black Mariah.* Evanston, IL: First Comics, 1987.

——. "Introduction." *Mister X: Condemned.* By Dean Motter, 7–8. Milwaukie, OR: Dark Horse, 2009.

Chinatown. Directed by Roman Polanski. Hollywood: Paramount, 1974.

Collins, Max Allan. "Dick Tracy Begins." *The Complete Chester Gould's* Dick Tracy: *Dailies and Sundays* 1931–1933. By Chester Gould, 2–5. San Diego: IDW, 2009.

Collins, Max Allan and Terry Beatty. *Ms. Tree.* New York: PaperJacks, 1988.

Collins, Max Allan and Lynn F. Myers. "Introduction: I, the Writer." *Byline: Mickey Spillane.* Edited by Max Allan Collins and Lynn F. Myers, 9–19. Norfolk, VA: Crippen and Landru, 2004.

Conard, Mark T. "*Reservoir Dogs*: Redemption in a Postmodern World." *The Philosophy of Neo-Noir.* Edited by Mark T. Conard, 101–16. Lexington: University Press of Kentucky, 2007.

Costello. Brannon. *Howard Chaykin: Conversations.* Jackson: University Press of Mississippi, 2011.

Craig, Johnny. "Dead-Ringer." *Crime SuspenStories* 2. New York: EC. December 1950.

——. "The Execution." *Crime SuspenStories* 12. New York: EC. August 1952.

The Crying Game. Directed by Neil Jordan. London: Palace Pictures, 1992.

The Dark Knight. Directed by Christopher Nolan. Burbank, CA: Warner Bros., 2008.

Dean, Michael. "The Brian Michael Bendis Interview." *The Comics Journal* 266 (Feb./Mar. 2005): 95–134.

Demott, Benjamin. "Darkness at the Mall: The 'New Wave' in Adult Comic Books Features Defeat, Cynicism, and Despair." *Psychology Today*, February 1984: 48–52.

Dial M for Murder. Directed by Alfred Hitchcock. Burbank, CA: Warner Bros., 1954.

Double Indemnity. Directed by Billy Wilder. Paramount, 1944.

Doyle, Sir Arthur Conan. "A Study in Scarlet." *The Annotated Sherlock Homes*. Edited by William S. Baring-Gould, 143–234. New York: Clarkson S. Potter, 1967.

Duncan, Randy and Matthew Smith. *The Power of Comics: History, Form, and Culture*. New York: Continuum, 2009.

Durgnat, Raymond. "Paint It Black: The Family Tree of Film Noir." *Film Noir Reader*. Edited by Alain Silver and James Ursini, 37–51. New York: Limelight Editions, 1996.

Eisner, Will. "The Killer." *The Best of* The Spirit. By Will Eisner, 51–58. New York: DC Comics, 2005.

——. "Meet P'Gell." *The Best of* The Spirit. By Will Eisner, 43–50. New York: DC Comics, 2005.

Ekstrom, Steve. "Exploring the Joker: Brian Azzarello Talks." *Newsarama*. Last modified October 2, 2008. http://www.newsarama.com/comics/090802-AzzarelloJoker.html.

Evans, Eric. "*100 Bullets*: Axel Alonso, Brian Azzarello. Dave Johnson, Eduardo Risso." The Comics Journal 228 (October 2000): 89–101.

Feldstein, Al. "The Law's Revenge." *War Against Crime* 5. New York: EC. February–March 1949.

Feldstein, Al and George Roussos. "The Escaped Maniac!" *Crime SuspenStories* 8. New York: EC. December–January 1951.

Feldstein, Al and Jack Kamen. "Only Skin Deep." *Shock SuspenStories* 13. New York: EC. March 1954.

——. "The Orphan." *Shock SuspenStories* 14. New York: EC. May 1954.

Feldstein, Al and Wally Wood. "Death's Double-Cross." *Crime SuspenStories* 1. New York: EC. October–November 1950.

——. "Faced with Horror." *Crime SuspenStories* 3. New York: EC. February–March 1951.

——. "The Whipping." *Shock SuspenStories* 14. New York: EC. May 1954.

Fox, Gardner and Bob Kane. "Batman Versus the Vampire." *The Greatest Batman Stories Ever Told*. Edited by Dick Giordano, 17–36. New York: DC Comics, 1988.

Frank, Nino. "A New Police Genre: The Criminal Adventure." Trans. Alain Silver. *Film Noir Reader 2*. Edited by Alain Silver and James Ursini, 15–19. New York: Limelight Editions, 1999.

Frankenstein. Directed by James Whale. Universal City, CA: Universal, 1931.

The G-Men. Directed by William Keighley. Burbank, CA: Warner Bros., 1935.

Gabilliet, Jean-Paul. *Of Comics and Men: A Cultural History of American Comic Books*. Translated by Bart Beatty and Nick Nguyen. Jackson: University of Mississippi Press, 2010.

Gardiner, Dorothy and Katherine Sorley Walker. *Raymond Chandler Speaking*. Berkeley: University of California Press, 1997.

George, Milo. *Frank Miller: The Interviews: 1981–2003*. Seattle: Fantagraphics, 2003.

Gibson, William. *Neuromancer*. New York: Ace, 2004.

Gilbert, James. *A Cycle of Outrage: America's Reaction to Juvenile Delinquent in the 1950s*. New York: Oxford University Press, 1986.

Goodstone, Tony. T*he Pulps: Fifty Years of American Pop Culture*. New York: Chelsea House, 1973.

Groth, Gary and Robert Fiore. *The New Comics: Interviews from the Pages of The Comics Journal*. New York: Berkley, 1988.

Haining, Peter. *The Classic Era of American Pulp Magazines*. Chicago: Chicago Review Press, 2000.

Hajdu, David. *The Ten Cent Plague: The Great Comic Book Scare and How It Changed America*. New York: Farrar, Straus, and Giroux, 2008.

Hammett, Dashiell. *The Maltese Falcon*. New York: Vintage, [1930] 1989.

——. *Red Harvest*. New York: Vintage, [1929] 1989.

Harvey, R.C. "When Less Is More, An Entire City: An Introduction." *The Art of Sin City*. By Frank Miller, 1–4. Milwaukie, OR: Dark Horse, 2002.

Hirsh, Foster. *Detours and Lost Highways: A Map of Neo-Noir*. New York: Limelight, 1999.

Haut, Woody. *Neon Noir: Contemporary American Crime Fiction*. London: Serpent's Tail, 1999.

——. *Pulp Culture*. London: Serpent's Tail, 1996.

Highsmith, Patricia. *Stangers on a Train*. New York: w.w. Norton, [1950] 2001.

Hirsh, Foster. *Detours and Lost Highways: A Map of Neo-Noir*. New York: Limelight, 1999.

Hudson, A. "Interview with Max Allan Collins." *Comic Attack*. Last updated June 3, 2012. http://comicattack.net/2012/06/invmaxallancollins/.

Hunter, Evan. *The Blackboard Jungle*. New York: Pocket, [1954] 2004.

Hunter, Evan and Ed McBain. *Candyland: A Novel in Two Parts*. New York: Simon and Schuster, 2001.

Invasion of the Body Snatchers. Directed by Don Siegel. Los Angeles: Allied Artist Pictures, 1956.

Irving, Christopher. "Brian Azzarello on Crime and Superheroes." *Graphic NYC*. Last modified October 26, 2011. http://www.nycgraphicnovelists.com/2011/10/brian-azzarello-on-crime-and.html.

Jenkins, Henry. "The Future Isn't What It Used to Be: An Interview with Comics Creator Dean Motter." *Confessions of an Aca-Fan*. Last modified June 6, 2007. http://henryjenkins.org/2007/06/an_interview_with_comics_creat.html.

——. "'The Tomorrow That Never Was'–Retrofuturism in the Comics of Dean Motter." *Comics and the City: Urban Space in Print, Picture, and Sequence*. Edited by Jorn Ahrens and Arno Meteling, 63–83. New York: Continuum, 2010.

Kane, Gil. *His Name Is… Savage.* New York: St. John Publications, 1968.

Kavanaugh, Dan. *Duffy*. New York: HarperCollins, [1980] 1989.

Kirby, Jack. *In the Days of the Mob* 12. New York: Hampshire Distributors (DC Comics). 1971.

A Kiss Before Dying. Directed by Gerd Oswald. Los Angeles: United Artists, 1956.

Kiss Me Deadly. Directed by Robert Aldrich. Los Angeles: United Artists, 1955.

Klaehn, Jeffrey. "Mister M: A Career Retrospective with Dean Motter." *Graphic Novel Reporter*. Last Modified June 25, 2011. http://graphicnovelreporter.com/content/mister-m-career-retrospective-dean-motter-interview.

Leonard, Elmore. *52 Pickup*. New York: HarperTorch, [1974] 2002.

——. *Get Shorty*. New York: Harper, [1990] 2005.

The Last Seduction. Directed by John Dahl. United Kingdom: Incorporated Television Company, 1994.

M. Directed by Fritz Lang. Berlin: Nero-Film AG, 1931.

The Maltese Falcon. Directed by John Huston. Burbank, CA: Warner Bros., 1941.

The Manchurian Candidate. Directed by John Frankenheimer. Los Angeles: United Artists, 1962.

Mayer, Geoff and Brian McDonnell. *Encyclopedia of Film Noir*. Santa Barbara: Greenwood, 2007.

McCue, Greg S. and Clive Bloom. *Dark Knights: The New Comics in Context*. London: Pluto Press, 1993.

Merivale, Patricia. "Gumshoe Gothics: Poe's 'The Man of the Crowd' and His Followers." *Detecting Texts: The Metaphysical Detective Story from Poe to Postmodernism*. Edited by Patricia Merivale and Susan Elizabeth Sweeny, 101–16. Philadelphia: University of Pennsylvania Press, 1999.

Metropolis. Directed by Fritz Lang. Berlin: Universum Film, 1927.

Miller, Frank. "Anarchy." *Frank Miller Homepage*. Last modified November 7, 2011. http://frankmillerink.com/.

——. *Batman: The Dark Knight Returns*. New York: DC Comics, 1996.

——. *Batman: Year One*. New York: Marvel Comics, 2001.

——. *Daredevil: Born Again*. New York: Marvel Comics, 2001.

——. *Daredevil: Visionaries 2*. New York: Marvel Comics, 2001.

——. *Daredevil: Visionaries 3*. New York: Marvel Comics, 2001.

——. *Hard Boiled*. Milwaukie, OR: Dark Horse, 2000.

——. *Ronin*. New York: DC Comics, 1987.

——. *Sin City: The Big Fat Kill*. Milwaukie, OR: Dark Horse, 2005.

——. *Sin City: A Dame to Kill For*. Milwaukie, OR: Dark Horse, 1995.

——. *Sin City: Family Values*. Milwaukie, OR: Dark Horse, 1997.

——. *Sin City: The Hard Goodbye*. Milwaukie, OR: Dark Horse, 1993.

——. *Sin City: Hell and Back*. Milwaukie, OR: Dark Horse, 2005.

——. *Sin City: That Yellow Bastard*. Milwaukie, OR: Dark Horse, 2005.

——. "That Old Piece of Cloth." NPR: "This I Believe." Last modified September 11, 2006. http://www.npr.org/templates/story/story.php?storyId=5784518.

Miller's Crossing. Directed by Joel Coen. Los Angeles: 20th Century Fox, 1990.

Mitchell, Elvis. "Frank Miller Interview on SoCal's KCRW." *Comic Book Resources*. Last modified March 30, 2005. http://www.comicbookresources.com/?page=article&id=4820.

Monaco, Paul. *John Dahl and Neo-Noir: Examining Auteurism and Genre*. Lanham, MD: Lexington, 2010.

Morcock, Michael, "Introduction," *American Flagg!: Hard Times*. By Howard Chaykin, 1–2. Evanston, IL: First Comics 1985.

Morgan, Jeffrey. "Motivation by Obsession: The Architect and the Archetype." Mister X: *The Definitive Collection*, Vol. 2. By Dean Motter, 6–9. New York: Simon and Schuster, 2005.

Morisi, Pete. "An Eye for an Eye." *Dynamite* 4. Comic Media. 1953.

Morton, Paul. "An Interview with Brian Michael Bendis." *Bookslut*. Last modified February 2009. http://www.bookslut.com/features/2009_02_014023.php.

Motter, Dean. Mister X: *The Definitive Collection*, Vol. 1. New York: Simon and Schuster, 2004.

———. Mister X: *The Definitive Collection*, Vol. 2. New York: Simon and Schuster, 2005.

Murder, My Sweet. Directed by Edward Dmytryk. New York: RKO, 1944.

Nash, Jesse W. "Gotham's Dark Knight: The Postmodern Transformation of Arthurian Mythos." *Popular Arthurian Traditions*. Edited by Sally K. Slocum, 36–45. Bowling Green: Bowling Green State Popular Press, 1992.

Nyberg, Amy. *Seal of Approval: The History of the Comics Code*. Jackson: University Press of Mississippi, 1998.

Palmer, R. Barton. *Hollywood's Dark Cinema: The American Film Noir*. New York: Twayne Publishers, 1994.

Phipps, Keith. "Interview: Brian Michael Bendis." *The Onion*. Last modified August 9, 2007. http://www.avclub.com/articles/brian-michael-bendis,14138/.

Pizzino, Christopher. "Art That Goes Boom: Genre and Aesthetics in Frank Miller's *Sin City*." *English Language Notes* 46 (November, 2008): 115–28.

Poe. Edgar Allan. "The Murders in the Rue Morgue." *The Gold Bug and Other Tales*. By Edgar Allan Poe, 30–56. New York: Dover, [1841] 1991.

Prescott, Peter S. "The Comic Book (Gulp!) Grows Up." *Newsweek* January 18, 1988, 70–71.

The Public Enemy. Directed by William Wellman. Burbank, CA: Warner Bros., 1931.

Pulp Fiction. Directed by Quentin Tarantino. New York: Miramax, 1994.

Rear Window. Directed by Alfred Hitchcock. Hollywood: Paramount, 1954.

Rebel without a Cause. Directed by Nicholas Ray. Burbank, CA: Warner Bros., 1955.

Red Rock West. Directed by John Dahl. Universal City, CA: Polygram, 1993.

Rich, James S. "Review: *Time2: The Epiphany*; *Time2: The Satisfaction of Black Mariah*." *Trouble with Comics*. Last modified December 2010. http://troublewithcomics.com/post/490426056/guest-reviewer-month-jamie-s-rich-on-howard.

Rodman, Larry. "New Blood: A Frank Miller Career Overview." *Frank Miller: The Interviews: 1981–2003*. Edited by Milo George, 121–31. Seattle: Fantagraphics, 2003.

Rope. Directed by Alfred Hitchcock. Burbank, CA: Warner Bros., 1948.

Rose, Lloyd. "Comics Books for Grow-Ups." *The Atlantic Monthly*, August 1986: 77–80.

Sacks, Ethan. "*100 Bullets*, Brian Azzarello and Eduardo Risso's Acclaimed Crime Comic Series, Ends with a Bang." *The New York Daily News*. Last modified April 15, 2009. http://articles.nydailynews.com/2009-04-15/entertainment/17920871_1_comic-books-super-heroes-vertigo-comics.

Sava, Oliver. "Interview: Ed Brubaker." *The Onion*. Last modified July 20, 2011. http://www.avclub.com/articles/ed-brubaker,59143/.

Scarlet Street. Directed by Fritz Lang. Universal City, CA: Universal, 1945.

Schumer, Arlen. "Introduction." Mister X: *The Definitive Collection*, Vol. 1. By Dean Motter, 9–14. New York: Simon and Schuster, 2004.

Schwartz, Richard B. *Nice and Noir: Contemporary American Crime Fiction*. Columbia, MO: University of Missouri Press, 2002.

Schwartz, Ronald. *Neo-Noir: The New Film Noir Style from* Psycho *to* Collateral. Lanham, Maryland: The Scarecrow Press, 2005.

Silver, Alain and Elizabeth Ward. *Film Noir.* New York: Overlook, 1992.

Singh, Arune. "Just the Facts Ma'am: Max Collins Talks Road to Perdition." *Comic Book Resources.* Last modified June 16. 2002. http://www.comicbookresources.com/?page=article&id=1193.

Smith, Erin A. *Hard-Boiled: Working-Class Readers and Pulp Magazines.* Philadelphia: Temple University Press, 2000.

Spurgeon, Tom. "A Short Interview with Ed Brubaker." *The Comics Reporter.* Last modified Aug 26, 2006. http://www.comicsreporter.com/index.php/resources/interviews/5964/.

——. "CR Sunday Interview: Ed Brubaker." *The Comics Reporter.* Last modified June 6, 2011. http://www.comicsreporter.com/index.php/cr_sunday_interview_ed_brubaker2012summer/.

——. "The Ed Brubaker Interview." *The Comics Journal* 263 (October–November, 2004): 59–99.

Steranko, Jim, Chandler: *Red Tide. Illustrated Fiction 3.* New York: Pyramid, 1976.

Thompson, Jim. *The Killer Inside Me.* New York: Vintage, [1952] 1991.

Tipton, Nathan G. "Gender Trouble: Frank Miller's Revision of Robin the *Batman: Dark Knight Series.*" *The Journal of Popular Culture* 41 (2008): 321–36.

Tuska, George. "Charles Barrone, the Murderous Bully." *Crime Does Not Pay* 53. New York: Lev Gleason. July 1942.

Ursini, James. "Noir Science." *Film Noir Reader 2.* Edited by Alain Silver and James Ursini, 222–41. New York: Limelight Editions, 1999.

Vertigo. Directed by Alfred Hitchcock. Hollywood: Paramount, 1958.

Vidler, Anthony. *The Architectural Uncanny: Essays in Modern Unhomely.* Cambridge: MIT, 1992.

Wagner, Geoffrey. P*arade of Pleasure: A Study in Popular Iconography in the USA.* New York: Library Publishers, 1955.

Wertham, Fredric. *Seduction of the Innocent.* Laurel, New York: Main Road Books, 2004.

Wiater, Stanley and Stephen R. Bisette. *Comic Book Rebels of the New Comics: Conversations with the Creators.* New York: Dutton, 1993.

Willett, Ralph. *The Naked City: Urban Crime Fiction in the USA.* Manchester: Manchester University Press, 1996.

Worley, Rob M. "Max Allan Collins Brings 'Ms. Tree' to Novels and TV." *Mania.* Last modified January 24, 2008. http://www.mania.com/max-allan-collins-brings-ms-tree-to-novels-tv_article_90640.html.

Wright, Bradford W. *Comic Book Nation: The Transformation of Youth Culture in America.* Baltimore: Johns Hopkins University Press, 2001.

Zalben, Alex. "Interview: Ed Brubaker Tells Us Why the New *Criminal* Is the 'Ultimate Crime Comic.'" *MTV.com.* Last modified June 1, 2011. http://geek-news.mtv.com/2011/06/01/interview-ed-brubaker-tells-us-why-the-new-criminal-is-the-ultimate-crime-comic/.

INDEX

Page numbers in italics indicate illustrations

A

C

D

E

F

G

H

I

J

N

S

T

U

V

W

Y

Z

COLOPHON

Molly Q. Cort
Editor

Bruce Ian Meader
Designer

Marnie Soom
Production

Adobe Caslon Pro, Neutraface 2
Typefaces

Endurance Silk
Text and Cover Paper

Global Printing
Alexandria, Virginia
Printer

This book was made possible, in part, through the generosity of Global Printing.